Dances With Werewolves

Dances With Werewolves

Paul Buchanan

Created by Paul Buchanan and Rod Randall

BROADMAN
& HOLMAN
PUBLISHERS
Nashville, Tennessee

© 2000 by Paul Buchanan
Printed in the United States of America

0–8054–1982–9

Published by Broadman & Holman Publishers, Nashville, Tennessee
Editorial Team: Vicki Crumpton, Janis Whipple, Kim Overcash
Page Composition: SL Editorial Services

Dewey Decimal Classification: Fiction
Subject Heading: CHRISTIAN FICTION—JUVENILE FICTION
Library of Congress Card Catalog Number: 99–048294

All Scripture quotations are from The Holy Bible, New International
Version (NIV) © 1973, 1978, 1984 International Bible Society; used by
permission.

Library of Congress Cataloging-in-Publication Data
Buchanan, Paul, 1959–
      Dances with werewolves / Paul Buchanan.
         p.   cm.—(Heebie Jeebies series ; v. 8)
      Summary: Because he is convinced that his camp coun-
selor is a werewolf, twelve-year-old Derek gets involved
in scary adventures but also learns to trust in the protection of God.
    ISBN 0–8054–1982–9 (pbk)
    [1. Camps—Fiction. 2. Werewolves—Fiction. 3. Christian
life—Fiction. 4. Horror stories.] I. Title. II. Series.
PZ7.B87717 Dan 2000
[Fic]—dc21   99-048294
                                          CIP

1 2 3 4 5 04 03 02 01 00

DEDICATION

For Jesse Ingraffia

Prologue

The crickets outside suddenly stopped chirping. I sat up on my bunk in the darkness and rubbed my eyes. My heart started racing. "Not again," I whispered. "This can't be happening. I'm just dreaming."

But it wasn't a dream, and I knew it.

I kneeled on my bunk and looked through the small window at the pine trees lit up silvery in the moonlight. I held my breath and waited. Then it began. It was a lonesome moan at first, far out in the woods. Soon it became a mournful, faltering howl that wound creepily through the trees.

The sound made my stomach twist with dread.

I glanced over at the door to make sure the brass bolt lock was in place. Scrunching back down on my bunk, I put my trembling fingers in my ears and hummed quietly to drown out the noise. But I could still hear the howling. I was not a happy camper.

1

Chapter 1

I looked out the car window. Pine trees whizzed by on the winding mountain road. They looked just like all the other pine trees we'd been driving through for the past hour. I tried the car radio, but all I got was static, so I switched it off. I rolled the window down a little and sniffed the clean mountain air everyone's always talking about.

"Everything up here smells like sawdust," I told my mom. "Is that how it's supposed to smell?"

Mom just laughed. I rolled the window up again.

I'm twelve, and twelve is old enough to take care of myself, but I've got to admit that the prospect of spending a month at a camp in the boonies makes me nervous. What if I don't make any friends? What if the other kids are mean to me? What if I get homesick? What if I get lost in the woods? I felt a lump growing in my throat.

My trip to Teepee Village Summer Camp is the first time I've really been away from home. Sure, I've been to a few sleepovers at friends' houses, and I've stayed at my grandmother's house a couple of weeks. But this is different. At Teepee Village, I'm going to be on my own.

Mom says I'm going to have the time of my life. She says I'll get over my homesickness before I know it. She insists I'll have more fun at summer camp than I would lying around the house watching television all day. She predicts I'll make life-long friends. I don't know about that.

This is also the first time I've really been out in the boonies. I live in the city and the closest thing to camping I've ever done is a picnic in the park.

"There's nothing to worry about," Mom said, as if she could read my mind. "You'll have a great time. By tomorrow afternoon you'll know plenty of people. The boys in your teepee will seem like old friends before you know it."

I looked out the window again. The woods were thick and dark and mossy. "Are there any bears up here?" I asked Mom.

"Not in these hills," she said.

"Any mountain lions or rattlesnakes?"

Mom smiled. "Nope. It's perfectly safe. There are no dangerous animals in these parts." She glanced over at me, her eyes sparkling. I could tell she was thinking that I was still her little boy. I could tell she wanted to reach over and muss my hair. "This will be good for you," she assured me. "You'll finally get acquainted with nature."

"I know plenty about nature," I told her. "We get it on cable."

Mom laughed. "Yeah, you're a real woodsman, you are."

"Any hyenas up here?" I asked. "Man-eating sharks?"

Mom laughed again. "Like I said: There are no dangerous animals in these woods."

Boy, was she ever wrong.

Chapter 2

An hour or so later, we saw the Teepee Village Summer Camp sign on the left side of the road. An arrow pointed to a narrow dirt road among the trees. The sign looked rickety and badly in need of paint. Mom slowed and turned onto the bumpy dirt road leading up to the camp.

We were a week late. The camp had started seven days ago, but our family had just gotten back from vacation. So when we finally reached the main parking lot, everything was in full swing. The gravel parking lot wasn't full of cars loaded down with luggage. Parents weren't saying good-bye to their kids. Counselors weren't toting clipboards and barking instructions. In fact, I could see only a handful of campers on the basketball and tetherball courts.

"Everyone must be down at the lake or at the swimming pool," Mom said. She knew about the lake and the swimming pool from the slick color brochure that had come in the mail. The brochure showed kids in canoes and on horseback, lush green lawns, and well-tended buildings.

But this place looked nothing like the brochure. Everything appeared run-down and faded. The buildings seemed rickety—like one strong gust of wind might blow them over. There was more dirt than grass on the ground, and what grass I saw was brown.

I could see only three cars in the gravel parking lot—all parked next to the building marked OFFICE. Mom pulled our red station wagon up next to a green one of the same make and model.

I got out of the car. It felt good to stand up after sitting for so long. A group of kids was playing horseshoes nearby. I watched them play while Mom looked for her purse. The kids either ignored me or didn't notice me. One of the players—a girl—was wearing a bright orange hat with earflaps, like something Elmer Fudd might wear.

Inside the office, we saw a door that had a window in the top half. Painted on the window, in neat gold letters, were the words CAMP DIRECTOR. Above that, someone's name, printed

in the same gold letters, had been scraped off.
MR. LUPINE had been written on the glass with a
Magic Marker.

"This is our first visit to Teepee Village," my
Mom told Mr. Lupine after we sat down in his
dimly lit office. "So we're not sure what we need to
do first." She sounded like she was planning to stay
at the camp as well. That would be fine with me.

Mr. Lupine looked down at some kind of chart
on his desk. "There's not much left to pick from,"
he murmured, thinking out loud. "We're almost
completely full. I think we may have to assign you
to the Andersons' teepee."

"The Andersons' teepee?" Mom said.

Mr. Lupine looked up suddenly. "Yes," he said,
a fake smile suddenly plastered on his face.
"They've been coming here for years." He pulled
at his nose thoughtfully. "We try to give them special accommodations."

Mom looked over at me and smiled. "You hear
that?" she said enthusiastically. "You get to stay
with the Andersons. You get special accommodations." I tried to smile.

While Mom was talking, I looked around the
office. It was dusty and bare. The sunlight stream-
ing between half-open blinds lit up swirling
streaks of dust in the air that made me want to

hold my breath. The paneled walls were covered with odd rectangles of darker stain where pictures must have once hung.

Mom kept talking, so I watched Mr. Lupine for a while. Something about him struck me as odd. While Mom talked, he seemed to be sniffing the air. At one point, he scratched behind his right ear—but not the way a normal person scratches. He had his head tilted way over and was going at it the way my cocker spaniel scratches at fleas, a weird look of concentration on his face. It kind of gave me the creeps.

"How long have you been the director here?" Mom asked, glancing around at the bare office walls.

"This is my first year as director," Mr. Lupine replied, a little too self-consciously. "I'm a local businessman, and I've been associated with this camp in one way or another for many years. So when the owner decided to sell, I jumped at the chance to expand my business holdings."

Mom nodded. I could tell what she was thinking: A new owner—*that's* why this place seems so run-down!

Mr. Lupine stood up and looked down at me. "If you'll just wait here a moment, I'll go get your

Teepee Village counselor," he told me. He disappeared out the door, leaving Mom and me alone in his office.

"The Anderson boys have been here before," Mom whispered when he was gone. "They can show you the ropes and introduce you around." Mom always tried to make the best of things.

I nodded.

Mr. Lupine came back in the room and took his place behind his desk. "Derek," he said smoothly. "I'd like you to meet your counselor, Slim."

Slim hovered in the doorway behind us. I looked back at him and smiled, but he didn't return my smile. He just stood there, avoiding eye contact.

It was easy to see where he got his name. He was tall and shockingly thin. He had sunken cheeks and a long, hooked nose. Prickly beard stubble stuck up all over his jaw. His face was so thin, it was hard to know how old he was. He could have been twenty-five or sixty-five; there was no telling.

"Slim, why don't you go unload Mrs. Thrasher's car?" Mr. Lupine suggested. "And then you can help young Derek take his things to his teepee."

Slim nodded and looked at my mom.

"It's the red Taurus station wagon," Mom told him. "I left it unlocked."

Slim nodded and shuffled down the hall.

Mom filled in all the forms and wrote Mr. Lupine a check. When we stepped out of the office into the bright light of day, we found Slim standing looking at the two station wagons parked next to each other. He hadn't unloaded my stuff yet.

"It's the red one," Mom called to him.

Slim didn't move.

"I'm afraid Slim and I are both color-blind," Mr. Lupine explained.

"Oh, I'm sorry," Mom said. "It's the car on the right."

Slim nodded and began unloading my things.

When the station wagon was empty, Mom closed the back door, got in and started the engine. I went around to the driver's side. She rolled the window down.

"You'll have a great time," Mom promised me again. "Slim seems like a very nice counselor, and the Anderson boys will be your best friends before the week is out." Like I said, she was trying to make the best of it.

She turned her head and tilted it for me to kiss her on the cheek. "Gotta go," she smiled. "You know where you can reach me, right?"

The car pulled away in a cloud of dust. I watched until it disappeared down the narrow dirt road among the tall pines.

When I turned, Slim was watching me. My two suitcases dangled at the end of his long, bony arms. I picked up my sleeping bag and followed him down a dirt path.

We passed plenty of teepee villages. Each village had four large teepees arranged around a big fire ring. Despite the run-down look of the rest of the camp, the teepees seemed in good repair. Each village was separated from the others by a stand of pine trees. Each time we came upon a new village along the trail, I assumed we'd be stopping, but we didn't. Slim kept leading me deeper and deeper into the woods.

Soon the trees grew so thick I had to stay close to Slim for fear of losing my way. Eventually we came upon another cluster of teepees huddled around a fire ring. They were more faded and run-down than any of the other ones we'd passed. This was where the trail ended. The tall trees out here loomed all around us—so tall and dark, it was hard to believe it was early afternoon.

Slim led me to one of the teepees. He put down one of my suitcases and pulled back the flap, so I could enter. I stepped inside the dark tent, hugging my sleeping bag.

It took a few seconds for my eyes to adjust to the dark. A few feet inside the tent flap, was an open wooden doorway. I walked through into a big round room, lined with bunk beds. It wasn't really a teepee at all inside. It was more like a ply-wood cabin with a creaky wooden floor and three high windows that let in very little light. A single bare light bulb dangled from the ceiling. In the darkness, I found the chain hanging from the bulb and pulled it. The teepee cabin was flooded with light.

There were six double bunks in the teepee—enough to hold a dozen campers—but only three of the bunks had sleeping bags on them. The three occupied bunks were all together, close to the door. The rest of the bunks had bare mat-tresses. I thought Mr. Lupine had said the camp was all booked up.

"You can pick any of the bunks you want," Slim told me from the doorway. I looked around.

"Which bunk is yours?" I asked.

"Oh, I don't sleep in here," Slim told me. "The counselor's teepee is just across the fire ring."

"You mean it's just kids in here?" I asked. Whatever happened to close adult supervision?

"Nothing to worry about," Slim said. "It's perfectly safe." He sounded like my mom.

"How many kids are in *your* teepee?" I asked.

"None," Slim replied. "You four boys are the only ones in this particular village." Something about this whole arrangement gave me the heebie jeebies.

I unrolled my sleeping bag on one of the unoccupied top bunks. I chose one close to the ones that already had sleeping bags. If I was going to be sleeping in this creepy teepee, with no adults around, I wanted to be close to the other campers. When I'd finished unrolling my sleeping bag, I set my pillow up at the head of the bed. I turned to ask Slim where the dining hall was, and when dinner would be served.

He was gone.

I didn't like this camp. I didn't like being out in the woods. I didn't like being in the teepee at the very end of the trail. I didn't like being in a half-empty cabin. I didn't like the fact that there'd be no adult in the teepee with us while we slept.

I put my two suitcases on the empty bunk below mine and went to the doorway. The door had a large brass lock screwed to the inside. It was the simple kind where you slide the bolt across into the brass eye on the doorframe. It seemed like a very large lock for such a small door. I went outside to look for Slim.

The fire pit in the middle of the circle of teepees was full of charred firewood and ashes, and it was surrounded by log benches. I looked at the other teepees. There were no signs of life. Which one was Slim's?

I went to the teepee next door. I stood outside the flap. How do you knock on a teepee? "Hello?" I called. "Hello? Anybody home?" No answer, just the wind moving through the tall pine trees.

I pulled the flap open. "Hello?" I called into the teepee. The door was open, and the cabin looked empty. I mean completely empty. There were no bunks or mattresses or anything. In the light coming through the door, I could see a layer of thick dust and pine needles covering the wooden floor. Cobwebs clung to the ceiling like a mist. Tiny paw prints, probably from rats, made crazy circles on the dusty floor.

I cringed and pulled the tent flap closed again. I *hate* rats! My skin crawled. I felt like washing my hands. I looked around the circle again. Am I all alone out here? I went to the next teepee over. It was empty too.

I went to the last teepee. It was on the opposite side of the fire from mine. I stood outside.
"Slim?" I called. "Are you in there?"

There was no answer.

I pulled back the flap. The door inside was
closed. I went in and knocked on the door. No
one answered. I pushed the door open, half
expecting to find another empty cabin, but it
wasn't empty. There was a big bed and a table
with four chairs. There was a dresser and a big
easy chair. This had to be Slim's teepee, but he
wasn't there.

I looked around the teepee from the doorway.
A few books and magazines were scattered on the
table, along with a big meaty bone. A bone?
Maybe Slim had a dog. The idea of having a
watchdog out here in the woods sounded good to
me.

From the doorway, I scanned the teepee for
other signs that a dog might live there. There
weren't any—no dog bed, no bowl, no leash, no
rawhide chew toys—just a big soup bone in the
middle of the table. I felt a sudden pang of dread,
though I wasn't sure why.

I pulled the door closed and went back outside. I looked around at our little teepee village
carved out of the forest. "Slim?" I called. I listened

to the sound of wind in the treetops. "Slim?" I called again, even louder. "Anyone here?"

No answer.

I looked down at my arm. I don't know if it was the brisk mountain air or the creepiness of the camp, but my skin was covered with goose bumps.

Somewhere out among the trees, I heard something move—just the scrambling of paws on dry pine needles. I felt a chill go up my spine. It was impossible to see very far into the forest. *It's just a squirrel,* I told myself. Or maybe a raccoon.

As I started up the narrow dirt path toward the main camp, I suddenly had the feeling that something was watching me from the forest.

Chapter 3

An hour later, a loud bell clanged somewhere. Everyone stopped what they were doing and lined up in front of a big building with double doors. I joined the line. I was pretty hungry, and I hoped the cafeteria would be a good place to meet some of the other campers. A group of girls talked and giggled in front of me in line. Behind me, a group of boys argued about the true winner of the diving competition they'd just held at the swimming pool.

I was near the front of the line, so when I got my tray of food—roast beef and mashed potatoes—there were still a lot of tables open. I took my tray and sat down at an empty table, hoping some friendly soul would soon join me and strike up a conversation. I bowed my head to say grace, and while I was talking to God, I asked Him to help me meet new people and not be too homesick.

Ten minutes later, the cafeteria was pretty much full, but the other seats at my table were still empty. The cafeteria was even louder than the one at school. Everyone seemed to be laughing and joking and talking—or maybe it just seemed that way because I was lonely. It looked like everyone had managed to form cliques before I got here.

I sat up straight and looked around. Way in the back of the cafeteria, I saw a large table with just three boys sitting at it. They were all huddled together, oblivious to the rest of us. Every other table, except for mine, was pretty much full.

I began eating. It was hard to swallow past the lump that was growing in my throat again. Conversations were going on all around me. A couple of times, in the midst of the general din of voices, I thought I heard someone say "the Awful Andersons," but I couldn't be sure.

A girl came toward me carrying a tray. It was the same girl I'd seen wearing the Elmer Fudd hat earlier. Only now the hat was tucked under her arm. She looked around at all the other tables, trying to spot an empty seat. Finally, she came over and stood beside me. "Is anyone else sitting here?" she asked.

"No," I said. "Help yourself." I gestured grandly at the vacant table.

The girl smiled and sat down. She bowed her head a few seconds. *She's a Christian,* I thought. I instantly felt more relaxed. I had someone to talk to. When she opened her eyes, she looked at me and smiled again.

"I was so late I didn't think I'd be able to find a seat," she told me.

"Not nearly as late as I was," I said. "I didn't even arrive at the camp until today."

"You just got here?" she asked. "Wow. Any news from the outside world? We're pretty cut off way up here."

"Not much news," I told her. "Just the war with Canada."

Her mouth fell open.

"I'm joking," I laughed. "We're not at war with Canada."

"You nearly gave me a heart attack," she scolded. "I have an aunt who lives in Calgary."

I grinned. "Well, as far as I know, we're still on good terms with our neighbors to the north." The girl was smiling now. I knew I'd made a friend.

"What village did they put you in?" she asked. "I'm in the Hopi village. My name's Kristen. Kristen Faulder." She reached out her hand for me to shake, so I did.

"I'm Derek Thrasher," I told her. "I'm not sure what village I'm in. Mr. Lupine just called it the Anderson Teepee."

Her mouth fell open again. She looked genuinely shocked. "You're with the *Andersons?*" she gasped. "Not the *Awful Andersons?*"

"I guess," I shrugged. "Mr. Lupine said they got special accommodations."

She laughed. "Yeah, it's called *solitary confinement.* Those boys are terrible. They're over there at the back table."

I glanced at the nearly empty table at the back. They were all huddled together still—a tight little group. "Really?" I said. "They're terrible? Like how?"

"They've done all kinds of things," Kristen said. "Rumor is, all the other counselors threatened to quit if they got assigned to the Andersons. They were in one of the boys' villages for the first few days, but they got moved out to some teepees that haven't been used for years. Mr. Lupine's brother was living out there by himself. So now he's supposed to be their counselor."

"So Slim isn't a real counselor?"

Kristen shook her head. "I've heard he just lives out there year round. So he ended up with the job." She held her finger and thumb out in front of her, about a quarter inch apart. "Everyone says Slim's this far from being a hermit. He *is* kind of creepy, if you ask me."

So I was trapped in a remote teepee village with three wild boys and a hermit? I had a lot to process. "So, Slim and Mr. Lupine are brothers?" I asked. "That explains why they're both color-blind."

"Half the staff at this camp are Mr. Lupine's relatives," Kristen said. "He bought the place last year and hired his whole family to work here."

"But the Andersons," I inquired. "What did they do to get put in solitary confinement?"

Kristen rolled her eyes. "What *didn't* they do?" she huffed. She looked up at the ceiling like she was doing math in her head. "First, they put live frogs in the water cooler. Then they invented some game where they try to capsize as many canoes on the lake as they can in one hour. Last week, they managed to sneak some bows and arrows out of the archery shed and shot down Mr. Lupine's remote control airplane."

I looked over at the three boys at the back table. They were leaning in close together, laughing and whispering—probably plotting something atrocious right now. I looked back at Kristen.

"They finally got moved to their own village when they trapped a live skunk under a wooden crate and tried to keep it as a pet," she told me. "It sprayed them and every other kid in their teepee. And it got a few of the counselors, too, before they managed to set it free."

She looked over at the Awful Andersons and then back at me. "Those boys are out of control," she warned. "You've got to get Mr. Lupine to move you."

"He said every other teepee was full."

"Then go home," Kristen told me. "If you know what's good for you, you'll call your Mom and beg her."

"I'm sure it won't be too terrible," I said hopefully. I was trying, like Mom, to see the best in the situation. "After all, I just have to *sleep* in the teepee. It's not like I have to hang out with them. When I make some friends up here I can—"

"Don't count on that," Kristen interrupted me. "Most of the kids up here just hang out with the people in their teepee village. It's like a bunch of cliques. I don't know a soul up here except the girls in my village."

"Not true," I corrected her. "You know me."

She smiled. "You're right. And now you have a friend up here too."

After dinner, we had a camp meeting. Mr. Lupine stood in front of the cafeteria and made some announcements into a microphone—including an announcement that seemed directed exclusively at the Andersons' table in the back about a missing fire extinguisher—and then he talked about different activities that would be available tomorrow.

When he was done with the announcements, Mr. Lupine handed out the mail. I kept looking back at the Andersons. They weren't even listening to hear if they had mail. They seemed immersed in some elaborate experiment involving table condiments and a bowl of chocolate pudding.

By the time the camp meeting was over, it was dark outside. I walked out of the cafeteria with Kristen. As soon as we got outside, she pulled on her Elmer Fudd cap. Taking a small flashlight from her pocket, she switched it on. It lit up a small oval of dirt at her feet. "I'm supposed to make hot chocolate for the girls in my village," she told me. "So I've got to get going. But I'll see you tomorrow." She took off down the trail toward the teepee villages, shining the flashlight in front of her.

"Yeah," I called after her. "Maybe I'll see you at breakfast."

"OK," she replied over her shoulder. "Good luck with the Awful Andersons."

For a few minutes, I could see her bright orange hat bobbing this way and that among the trees far along the trail. I was alone now, standing outside the cafeteria. I looked up at the stars. There were millions of them, and a huge full moon seemed to perch atop the pine trees across the way.

Usually when I look up at a night sky, crowded with stars, it makes me feel good. It makes me think of how big God is, and how He's got everything under control. But tonight the stars just made me feel lonely and small. I wished I could talk to my mom. I wished I was home in my own house. I wished I was anywhere but here.

I hadn't thought of bringing a flashlight when I packed my bags at home yesterday—like I said, I'd never been to camp before—and I knew it would be hard to find my way back to the Awful Andersons' teepee village on my own. So I hung out in front of the cafeteria doors, waiting for the Andersons to come out. I thought I'd introduce myself as their new teepee-mate, and then we could walk back together.

I kept searching the faces of the kids coming out the doors, hoping to recognize one of them. Kid after kid passed by in groups and pairs. None of them really looked at me. Pretty soon, the last few stragglers came out. Had I missed the Andersons?

I waited a minute or two, and when it seemed like no one else was coming out of the building, I slipped in through the door to look for the Andersons. There wasn't a kid in the place now— just Slim and one of the cooks, who was stacking up the empty serving trays.

"All I want is a doggie bag," Slim said. "Some of that beef would be good."

"Sure thing, Cuz," the cook said. "We've got plenty left over. How do you want it cooked?"

"Cooked?" Slim said. "I've got to have it raw."

The cook laughed. "Oh, yeah," the cook said. "I forgot who I was talking to."

The cook carried the empty serving trays through the swinging kitchen doors, with Slim following behind him.

Raw meat? I thought. It must be for his dog.

I slipped outside again and walked over to where the trail led into the woods. I didn't want to hike the trail alone in the dark. Since I'd missed the Andersons, I figured I'd wait for Slim and walk with him. He'd definitely have a flashlight. He kind of gave me the creeps, but it would be better than walking alone.

I stood near the top of the trail and waited until I saw Slim slip out through the cafeteria door with a package wrapped in butcher paper. He came walking toward where I stood in the shadows. Crickets chirped noisily all around me. But when Slim came near, everything fell eerily silent.

In the light of the full moon, he looked pale and ghostly. I felt the hairs on the back of my neck stand on end. When he neared me, I stepped back among the trees, out of the moonlight, where I wouldn't be seen. Suddenly, walking with Slim through the dark woods didn't seem like such a great idea.

I held my breath as he passed by, whistling a tune. It was "Blue Moon," one of the songs Mom always played on the piano and made me sing along with. It turned out that Slim didn't have a flashlight after all, but he strode confidently through the woods. I let him hike down the trail a ways and then fell in behind him.

I stayed close enough so I wouldn't lose him, but far enough back so he wouldn't notice me. Despite his color-blindness, he seemed to see very well in the dark. I struggled to keep up with him—stumbling and tripping on the uneven dirt path. The woods were oddly silent now. Not a single cricket chirped.

We passed the other teepee villages one after another. Each was crowded with kids around roaring campfires, roasting marshmallows and singing camp songs with their counselors. The windows of the teepees were lit up with lanterns. I sighed. Why couldn't I be in one of *those* villages?

We came to the last village before our own. The teepees there were all fixed up neatly and the whole site was landscaped and neatly maintained. The village was full of girl campers, and they seemed to be having a great time. I saw Kristen Faulder sitting on a log between two of the women counselors, sipping hot chocolate from a mug. All the girls' faces were lit up golden by the campfire light, and Kristen's orange hat glowed like a jack-o-lantern.

I paused for a moment, but I knew that Slim was slipping farther ahead, and I knew I'd better keep up with him if I didn't want to get lost in the woods. As soon as I stepped away from Kristen's village, it seemed as though the trail plunged into utter darkness. Even the full moon didn't filter through the thick trees. I couldn't really see Slim now. But I could hear him striding up ahead among the trees, whistling, and I did my best to follow the sounds he made.

After what seemed like a long time of stumbling along the black trail, I saw the dim flicker of firelight through the trees. As I got closer, I saw the three Anderson boys seated around a huge, roaring fire. How had they gotten past me?

"You must be the new kid," one of the Andersons said when I stepped into the circle of firelight. "It's about time someone moved in here."

I glanced around. Slim was nowhere in sight. I was kind of hoping he might introduce us—and maybe tell them to take it easy on me.

"I'm Derek," I said nervously. "Derek Thrasher. I just got here." I felt like I'd fallen into the gorilla enclosure at the zoo. I tried not to look scared.

"I'm Ryan," the biggest of the three boys said. "This is my kid brother, Nathan, and that's my cousin, Nic. Pull up a log."

"Nice to meet you," I said amiably. I went over and sat on an empty log across the fire from the three of them. The fire was so big, I had to sit well back on the log to keep my face from getting too hot. I looked around at the three faces lit up by firelight. Flames seemed to dance in their wide eyes.

I'm a good kid. I'm well-behaved. I've never been called into the principal's office. I think I've won every citizenship award my school ever invented. When I was a little kid, even my babysitters said I was an angel.

But now I'd been thrown to the lions. I was with the Awful Andersons. The kids who tried to keep a live skunk as a pet. The kids who were banished to the last teepee village on earth. The kids who didn't even have a real counselor. I was sitting on a log, but it felt like I should be strapping on a seat belt.

Chapter 4

I looked around at the teepee village in the fire-light. No wonder it was so run-down. No campers had probably lived in this part of the camp for years. And no wonder Slim didn't act like a camp counselor is supposed to act. He was just some old hermit living out here in the boonies at his brother's camp.

Nathan reached behind the log he was sitting on and threw another piece of wood on a fire that was already alarmingly large. I leaned back. Sparks flew high in the air, and I wondered how much it would take to burn the whole teepee village to the ground.

"Where did Slim go?" I asked, hoping we might get a little adult supervision—even if only from a hermit.

"He's in his teepee," Ryan said. "Why?"

"I don't know," I said. "Don't we do anything at night? All the other villages seemed to have activities with their counselors."

Ryan looked at the other two and laughed. "This isn't like the other villages," he smirked. "Slim keeps to himself mostly. We do too."

"So, we don't have any activities?" I asked.

"We make up our own activities," Nic replied.

So I'd heard.

Nathan put another log on the fire. I pulled my feet under me to keep them from roasting. They all started talking among themselves. I had no idea what they were talking about, so I tried to think of something to say that would get me in the conversation.

"What kind of dog does Slim have?" I asked when there was a lull in their conversation.

"Dog?" Nathan said. "Slim doesn't have a dog. But there's an old cat that comes around every once in a while."

"Is it Slim's cat?" I asked.

Ryan snorted a laugh. "Slim *hates* that cat," he said. "It drives him crazy."

"Every time that cat comes around, Slim takes off chasing after it," Nathan said. "He can't stand the thing."

I suddenly got a weird, nervous feeling in the pit of my stomach. I watched the roaring fire a while, trying not to think about the situation I was in. The Awful Andersons talked, but I paid no attention to what they were saying. I just kept staring at the fire, trying to think of pleasant things that would help me relax.

But my mind kept straying back to Slim. He was one weird guy. I could see why he'd end up way out here on his own—he was just too creepy to live anywhere normal. He was color-blind, chased cats, and wanted raw meat for some reason. An idea began to stir in my head, but my thinking was interrupted by something Ryan said.

He leaned forward, the fire dancing in his eyes. "I believe it's time to scare the living daylights out of each other," he announced.

"Time for a Terrifying Teepee Tale," Nic said, rubbing his palms together. "Whose turn is it to tell a story?"

Scary campfire tales. Just what I needed to round out the perfect day! I looked around at the three faces lit up by the campfire. I don't read a lot of scary books or go to horror movies—it's just not the kind of thing I enjoy. My heart beat faster. I didn't want to hear a scary tale out here in the middle of the woods. Just *being* here was creepy enough.

"*I've* got a scary story," Nic said. "But this one really happened."

"Cool," Nathan told him. Nathan put another log on the fire. Where did they get all this wood?

"This happened to my parents before I was born," Nic said. He looked at his two cousins. "They don't like to talk about it. So you can't tell them I told you."

Ryan and Nathan crossed their hearts elaborately and promised they would never tell, and if they did, their eyes would fall out and their livers would explode. Then they all looked at me. It wasn't like I was ever going to meet Nic's parents, but I promised never to tell them either. "My lips are sealed," I told them.

Nic stared into the fire. The flames flickered in his eyes as he began his story.

"My folks were driving along a lonely stretch of Ortega Highway on a dark and stormy night," he said eerily. "They were coming back from Lake Elsinore, and it was close to midnight. They were just driving and listening to the radio, but Dad noticed that the gas gauge was near empty, and they were miles from the next gas station.

"They drove as far as they could, and then the engine began to sputter, and then it cut out. Dad coasted over onto this dirt road, and managed to get the car off the highway. The rain was coming down hard, so they just sat in the car, listening to the radio, wondering what they could do. 'When the rain lets up a bit, I'll hike on down to the next gas station and get help,' Dad said to my mom. 'You can stay in the car.'

"The rain hammered down on the roof so hard they could barely hear the radio," Nic continued. "Just then, a news bulletin came on the radio: 'The sheriff's department has just announced that an inmate has escaped from the Capistrano Prison for the Criminally Insane. He's about six-foot-six, with shaggy black hair and a steel hook in the place of his right hand. If you see him, call the police immediately. Do not go near him. He is a deranged killer.'

"Not long after the news bulletin, the rain let up a little. 'I'm going to hike out to the gas station now,' Dad told Mom. 'Lock all the doors and don't open them for anyone.'

"'But you can't go out there,' Mom said. 'Didn't you hear what they said about the escaped guy with the hook? That prison is only a few miles from here.'

"'That's why we need gas,' Dad told her. 'We can't stay out here all night. The gas station's only a mile or so from here. I'll be back in half an hour. In an hour we'll be safe and dry in our own warm home.'

"Dad got out of the car and made sure Mom locked all the doors. He got an empty gas can out of the trunk, and took a tire iron for protection, and he started hiking down the dark highway toward the gas station.

"It was still drizzling and the wind was blowing, but Dad kept walking through the mist and the rain. Ten minutes later, he saw the lights of the gas station through the mist. He smiled and picked up his pace.

"When he got to the gas station, all the lights were on inside, but the door was locked. He banged on the door and an attendant peeked over the counter. 'I'm out of gas,' my Dad shouted. He held up the empty gas can.

"The gas station attendant stood up. He was pointing a shotgun at my Dad. 'Let me see your other hand,' he called through the closed glass door. Dad dropped the tire iron and raised his hand. The attendant pointed his shotgun at the floor. He came and opened the door.

"'Sorry about that,' the attendant said. 'But there's an escaped killer out here somewhere with a hook instead of a hand. When I saw you coming down the road holding that tire iron, I thought you were him.'

"Dad filled up the empty gas can and then asked the attendant if he'd give him a ride back up to the car. 'Not with that crazy guy out there,' the attendant said. 'I'm staying right here where there's light and a working phone.' So Dad started hiking back up Ortega Highway with the tire iron in one hand and the heavy gas can in the other.

"After a few minutes, the rain stopped, but it was still misty. No crickets were chirping because of all the rain, so the road was absolutely silent. The only sound was Dad's footsteps crunching along on the roadside gravel.

"Dad passed a grove of trees and heard something move deep among the branches. 'Probably just a squirrel or a crow,' he told himself, but he quickened his pace, anxious to get back to the car and get on his way.

"He was thinking about Mom waiting all alone in the car, when he noticed the echo. Every step he took, he heard an echo behind him. He stopped walking and spun around. He couldn't see very far in the mist, but the road behind him was silent. He stood a moment wondering what he should do. His breath clouded the air.

"Dad turned around and started walking. The echoing footsteps started up again. Every step he took on the gravel, he heard another step behind him. It had to be an echo, but his imagination was running wild. He kept glancing over his shoulder, but the fog was so thick now he couldn't see more than a few yards in any direction.

"He moved out to the middle of the road, hiking along the white line, so he wouldn't fall into a roadside ditch or walk into a tree branch. He just hoped he wouldn't pass right by his car in the fog.

"It occurred to him that the echoing footsteps were no longer behind him. They were off to the side. Dad was walking on the asphalt now, but the other footsteps seemed to be walking on gravel.

"Dad's mind raced. His heart pounded. He listened to the footsteps beside him in the fog. They didn't quite match up with his. Dad gripped the tire iron and took off running. He sprinted along the white line in the middle of the road as fast as he could, but it wasn't easy carrying the gas can full of gas.

"Dad ran as fast and hard as he could. He got a pain in his side, and he felt like his heart was going to explode. Then, when he couldn't run any longer, he came to a curve in the road and saw the faint outline of the car, off to the side, parked on the dirt road.

"Dad ran to the car. Mom unlocked the door. Dad jumped inside and slammed the door. He locked it. Mom hugged him crying. 'I was so worried,' she said. 'I kept imagining that crazy guy with the hook. I'm so glad you're all right.'

"Dad waited a while in the car. He was still pretty rattled, but he didn't want to worry Mom. He told her he was just catching his breath. He peered out the window, trying to see if anything was moving out in the fog.

"'Come on,' Mom begged him. 'Pour in the gas. I'm scared. Let's get out of here.'

"Dad slowly got out of the car, still holding the tire iron. He went to the gas cap, which was on his side. He inserted the nozzle of the gas can, and stared around him in the fog while the gas glugged into the tank. When the gas can was empty, he hurriedly put the gas cap back on and jumped into the car.

"He had to try the engine a few times before it would start. But as soon as the car started, he threw it in reverse and peeled out onto the highway and headed for home.

"As he drove home, he felt kind of foolish. He'd let his imagination run away with him. He'd been scared by his own echo.

"In half an hour, they were in town, and all the lights and people made them both relax. Dad had only put a gallon of gas in the car, so he pulled into a brightly lit gas station. He got out and started filling up the car. Mom told him she was going to find the rest room. She got out of the car and shut the door behind her. Then she let out a blood-curdling scream. Dad ran around to her side of the car."

Nic stopped talking. He looked around the circle at us, his eyes wide.

"That's when Dad knew for sure what had happened," he said breathlessly. "There, hanging from the door handle on Mom's side of the car, was a blood-smeared *steel hook*."

For a while the only sound was the roaring of the campfire.

I was pretty sure this *wasn't* a true story. It was just a campfire tale. In fact, I seemed to remember hearing a couple of stories just like it before. I'd even seen one on TV. But still, Nic claimed it *was* true.

I swallowed. The back of my neck tingled. I looked around at the dark trees that encircled us. Only the front few were lit up by the campfire. Who knew what might be watching us from the woods? I looked around at the trees, half expecting to see a steel hook suddenly glint in the light from the fire.

"*Cool,*" Nathan said.

"It *was* a cool story," Ryan said. "But I see one flaw in it."

"Yeah?" Nic said. "What's that?"

"There's no prison in Capistrano," Ryan said.

Nic thought for a moment. "They had to close it up because the crazy people kept escaping," he said. "There was some kind of secret tunnel."

"*Cool,*" Nathan said.

The huge fire crackled and roared.

"How did the guy expect to open the door with just a hook?" Ryan wanted to know. "It seems to me he'd open the door with his good hand and attack with his hook."

"Maybe both his hands were hooks," Nic suggested.

"*Cool,*" Nathan said.

The story didn't seem to faze the Awful Andersons a bit. I guess they were used to scary stories. But I sat perched on my log, alert and terrified, glancing this way and that at the dark woods surrounding us. Every time the fire spat sparks into the air, I jumped.

Chapter 5

I don't want to sound like a sissy, but lying on my bunk that night, I kept thinking about Nic's story. The teepee was very dark. The fire was out, the light was switched off, and the three Anderson boys were snoring away on their bunks. The full moon shone in through the window and left a pale rectangle of light on my sleeping bag.

I lay there thinking about how deep in the woods we were—how there was hardly anyone in this teepee village, how anyone or anything could be lurking right outside our teepee, and we'd never know it. I thought of the crazy guy with the hook. I knew the story wasn't true. I knew it was just a dumb campfire tale that people had probably been telling for fifty years. But still. Wasn't it *possible?*

Lying there in the dark, it was hard to know what to think. It was hard to keep my imagination from running wild. I sat up on my bunk and listened to the three Andersons breathing in the dark. I couldn't sleep. I would have felt better just to have the light on.

It's hard to sleep in a new place, especially when you're far away from your parents. It's hard to be among strangers. I opened and closed my fists and tried to relax. This camp seemed hostile and unfriendly. It seemed like I'd never feel at home here.

I thought I should probably read my Bible. That always gave me courage when I felt overwhelmed. I pulled it out from under my pillow and opened to Deuteronomy 31. I could just barely make out the words in the light of the full moon. This was one of my favorite Bible passages. The chapter tells how the children of Israel were going to enter a new and hostile land. Everyone was pretty nervous because Moses, their leader, wasn't coming with them. It was kind of like the situation I was in, but a hundred times scarier.

I got to verse six, my favorite: "Be strong and courageous. Do not be afraid or terrified because of them, for the Lord your God goes with you; He will never leave you nor forsake you."

I closed my Bible and settled back on my bunk. God was in control of everything; I knew I could rely on Him. I knew He was here in this dark teepee with me. I knew He was the God who created the universe. I had nothing to be afraid of.

Suddenly I wanted to look at the starry sky. Like I said, it always reminds me how great God is, and how He has everything under control. I crawled out of my sleeping bag and kneeled, looking out the window over my bed. The dark trees were too tall and too close to the teepee. I could just see a few scraps of sky here and there, and the glow of the full moon behind the tangled branches.

I slipped down off my bunk and tiptoed over to the door. The floor boards creaked a little, but the Andersons' breathing never changed. I just wanted to poke my head out and look up at the starry sky.

I pushed the door open and tiptoed over to the front flap of the teepee. Sticking my head out, I looked at the dark teepee village. The fire ring was still smoking and the smell of burning wood still hung in the air. On the other side of the fire pit, the flap to Slim's teepee was tied back, and his door stood wide open. The light was on inside. Was Slim still awake?

If the Israelites weren't afraid of the giants in the Promised Land they were entering, I figured *I* shouldn't be afraid of my own camp counselor. If he was still awake, maybe we could hang out a little. He probably wasn't so creepy once you got to know him. This might be my chance to make a friend.

I went back to my bunk and pulled on my shoes. I slipped out the door of the teepee and crossed over to Slim's. I stood outside his open door. "Slim?" I called in a half whisper. "You awake?" There was no answer. I stepped inside the flap and rapped on the doorjamb. "Slim?" I called again, a little louder.

I waited. Still no answer. I stepped into the open doorway. The light was on, but Slim wasn't there. I looked around the room. Some white butcher paper, streaked with juices and blood, lay empty on the table. He hadn't really *eaten* that meat raw, had he?

Just then I heard it. It came from the woods to my right—a high-pitched, mournful howl. It was like the sound my cocker spaniel makes when a fire truck passes by with its siren blaring—but somehow this howl was spookier and lonelier. I spun around and looked out at the dark campsite.

The howl came again, eerie and high pitched.

I froze in my tracks and listened. It's probably just a coyote, I told myself. Mom had told me there were no coyotes up here—but maybe she was wrong. Maybe she'd just told me that so I'd be more at ease.

I looked around in the dim moonlight. I was only twenty yards from my own teepee. I bent and picked up a stone, so I'd have something to throw if the coyote came out of the woods at me.

I took a few steps, and the sound came again. I froze and listened. I strained to see through the dark trees. First thing tomorrow, I resolved, I'd go to the camp store and buy the biggest flashlight I could find.

The howling stopped and I took a few more cautious steps toward my teepee, resisting the urge to run. I was almost there. A few more steps and I'd be safe inside.

And then it howled again, much closer this time. Just off to my left. I stopped dead in my tracks and snapped my head around. I held my breath and peered at the woods. I felt the breeze move through my hair.

And then I saw it. Two red eyes blinked in the darkness. Something large and black was watching me from the woods—its eyes glowing dimly in the moonlight. I heard a low growl. I squeezed the rock in my right hand. The thing snarled again, more throaty and menacing now.

I could just make out the dark shape of some large animal—much larger than the coyotes I'd seen on cable TV—watching me from the bushes.

I slowly pulled back the arm that held the rock. I've pitched in Little League for years. I have good aim. When the creature growled again, I threw the rock straight and hard—right at the two glowing eyes. I heard a thud, a sharp yelp and then an angry growl.

I sprinted to my teepee, dashed inside and pushed the door shut. I leaned against it, breathing hard, trying to slow my heart. I reached back and slid the brass bolt into place.

Out in the woods, I heard the howling begin again—now even more mournful. I crawled up on my bunk and lay there listening. I don't think I got a minute of sleep until the sun started shining through the window.

Actually, I must have dozed off, because the next thing I knew, I was alone in the teepee. The Andersons must have gone to breakfast without waking me. I crawled out of my sleeping bag and kneeled to look through the teepee window. The pine trees outside looked beautiful in the morning light. The sky was blue and sunny. It was hard to believe that this was the same place that had terrified me so much the night before.

I thought I should probably report what I had seen last night. If there was some kind of wild animal out there, Slim should probably know about it. What if it was something dangerous—like a mountain lion or a black bear?

I went over to Slim's teepee to see if he was in. I pulled back the flap and knocked on the door. Inside I heard some kind of grumble. Had he said *"Come in"?*

I slowly pushed the door open and poked my head inside. Slim lay in his bed, snoring loudly and grumbling in his sleep. I debated with myself, wondering if I should wake him. His hands and feet twitched fitfully under the covers, like he was having a dream.

I stepped into the room and closed the door quietly. I'd better wake him. I should definitely tell *someone* what I'd seen last night—and, odd though Slim *was,* he was my counselor.

I slipped up next to his bed, and was reaching out to shake his shoulder, when I looked at his face. There, on the left side of his forehead, was a large bruise, blue and swollen—exactly as if he'd been hit on the head with a rock.

I caught my breath. I pulled back my hand. My heart jackhammered in my chest, as I slowly backed toward the door. All kinds of ideas sped through my mind—raw meat, color-blindness, chasing cats, last night's full moon and now this bump on his head!

I slipped outside Slim's teepee and stood a moment looking down at the ash-covered fire pit. "Nah," I said aloud. I shook my head. "Impossible." I tried to laugh, but it sounded hollow in the mountain air. I looked back at Slim's teepee. *You know what?* I thought. *My cocker spaniel twitches like that when she's having a dream.*

Something strange was going on at this camp, and whatever it was, I didn't like it. A chill ran up the back of my neck. My mind settled on one impossible, terrifying word: werewolf! I shook my head, as if it might scatter the creepy thought. *Don't think like that,* I told myself.

I needed to talk to someone. But the only people I knew at this stupid camp were Slim and the Awful Andersons. I needed to talk to someone normal. And then it hit me. I *did* know someone normal—I knew Kristen Faulder.

I started down the trail toward the main camp. Kristen's village was the closest one to mine. It was just a few minutes' walk away. Maybe I could even talk to one of her counselors. They seemed pretty normal.

By the time I got to the girls' teepee village, I was already feeling better. I stepped into the clearing and looked around at the cluster of teepees. It was surprising to see it so quiet after all the activity I'd seen there last night. The flaps on the teepees were all tied back. One of the teepee doors was open. "Hello?" I called. I went over and peeked inside.

The teepee was empty. The bunks were all stripped. There was no luggage or clothing—no toothpaste tubes or towels. All I could see were some pine needles and sand scattered on the floor and one empty soda can.

I went to another teepee and knocked on the door. There was no answer. I pushed the door open. Another deserted teepee.

I tried the other two teepees. Both were empty.

I must have made some kind of mistake. This couldn't be the same village that was full of girls last night. I must have walked by this empty village in the dark without knowing it was there. But deep down I *knew* this was Kristen's teepee village. I walked over to the fire pit and squatted beside it. I held my palm low over the ashes and blackened logs. The fire pit was still warm. There had definitely been a fire here last night.

I stood up and looked around. If this was Kristen's campsite, where was Kristen? And where were all the other girls I'd seen here? It wasn't like they'd just gone to breakfast—all their stuff was gone. They'd disappeared.

I thought about Kristen in her orange hat with the earflaps. I thought about the glowing eyes I'd seen in the dark woods. I thought about Slim lying in his bed right now with a bump on his head. And then I gave voice to my deepest fear.

"Werewolf!"

Chapter 6

I had to do something. This was a state of emergency. All the pieces fit together. Everything added up. But I was the only one who knew. Slim was some kind of werewolf, and he'd eaten an entire teepee village of campers.

No sooner had the thought registered than I felt like a complete idiot. I blushed and looked around the deserted village. My imagination was running away with me. This was my first time away from home. I was nervous and my mind was running wild. I had to rein myself in.

"Will you listen to yourself," I said aloud, standing next to the smoldering fire pit. "You have lost your mind. You can't possibly believe that Slim is a werewolf. Sure, he's a little weird, but he's no monster." I knew I was right.

But another part of my mind was still ill at ease. "Well then, *you* explain it. Give me a plausible explanation for all this," I said aloud. "You saw it all. How can you say I'm crazy?"

The other part of my mind took over again. "Well, first of all, you're standing here talking to yourself out loud," I said.

It was a good point. I blushed again and looked around at the empty campsite. *Regroup*, I told myself. *You're under a lot of stress. Go have breakfast. You'll find Kristen and realize this was all a mistake.*

But I didn't see Kristen at breakfast, and I didn't see her at lunch. I walked all over camp that afternoon—out to the lake, up to the archery shed, down past the swimming pool. That orange Elmer Fudd cap was hard to miss, but I didn't see it anywhere. I visited every teepee village up and down the trail, trying to see if I'd made some mistake last night—but I hadn't. That was definitely Kristen's teepee village, and it was definitely deserted.

Around four in the afternoon, I remembered to go to the camp store to buy a flashlight. I certainly didn't want to be walking around in the dark without one tonight. The store was only open from three o'clock until the dinner bell rang, so I headed over to that side of camp. When I came through the door, the Awful Andersons were in the store already, rummaging through a basket full of squirt guns. The squirt guns were right next to the rack of flashlights.

I was about to step back outside, when Ryan saw me. "There you are, David," he said. "Where have you been hiding?"

There was no escaping them now. "Oh, I've just been hanging around," I said, forcing a smile. "And my name's not David. It's Derek." I glanced around the store. It was really just a medium-size room with three narrow aisles running the length of it. I started down the aisle farthest from the Andersons and pretended to look at a tube of toothpaste.

"You should have been with us, today," Nic called over to me enthusiastically. "We invented a way to catch fish with a garden hose and a bunch of firecrackers."

"Gee," I said. "I'm sorry I missed it." I don't think I said it convincingly.

"We didn't actually catch any fish," Nic admitted. "But we blew the garden hose up pretty good."

I didn't know what to say. I just kept the dopey grin plastered on my face and nodded.

"Why don't you come along with us now?" Ryan asked. He seemed to be the leader of the group.

This was the first time anyone at this camp had invited me to do anything. Maybe the Andersons weren't so awful after all. "Where are you guys going?" I asked.

Ryan pointed a purple squirt gun at the ceiling. "We just found a hornets' nest," he said. "We're going to shoot it with vinegar and see what happens."

The fake smile stayed plastered on my face. "Maybe some other time." I said.

"Suit yourself," Ryan shrugged.

I got to the cafeteria early for dinner and sat near the door so I could watch every single person who came in. I thought maybe I'd just missed Kristen Faulder earlier when I'd looked for her all over camp. Maybe she'd stopped wearing that orange hat. Maybe she'd walked right by me without my even noticing. I checked each face that passed through the cafeteria doors. None of them was Kristen's.

When I was done eating, I scanned the cafeteria. The Awful Andersons were alone at their usual table at the back. Their faces and arms were dotted with white lotion now, but it didn't seem to bother them any. They were huddled together again, oblivious to the rest of us, no doubt plotting some other stunt.

Aside from the empty spaces at the Anderson's table, it seemed like there were a lot more empty chairs throughout the cafeteria than last night. There was no other way to explain it—there weren't as many campers here tonight.

I watched all the other kids talking and laughing. Was I the only one to notice the absences? Was everyone else so wrapped up in their summer camp cliques? Did no one else even realize an entire teepee village had vanished?

When the meal was over, Mr. Lupine stood at the front of the cafeteria to make his announcements. I didn't really listen to what he was saying. Instead, I watched him closely as he talked into the microphone. Was it my imagination, or did he seem a little nervous? His eyes darted around the room as he spoke. There was a weird, anxious flutter in his voice. Did he know about the missing campers? Was he trying to cover up for his brother, Slim?

The camp meeting split up early. While everyone else filed out of the cafeteria, I stayed put. I sat in my chair until the last kids left the cafeteria.

I wanted to talk to Mr. Lupine alone. He was up front now, talking to a couple of cafeteria workers. As he talked, he glanced over at me a few times, no doubt wondering why I was still sitting there. When the two staff members headed for the door, I stood up and walked over to Mr. Lupine.

"Derek," he said as I approached. "I know why you're here. But you've got to understand that we're full up this year. We were fortunate to find a place for you at all. It would be impossible to move you." I felt like telling him there was a whole teepee village completely empty now—so there should be plenty of room. But I held my tongue.

"That's not why I'm here," I told him.

He seemed surprised. "Really?" he said. "It's not? What is it you want then?"

"I just came to tell you that your brother, Slim, seems to be hurt," I said. "He had a big bump on his head this morning."

Mr. Lupine glanced around nervously, as if to see if anyone might be listening, but we were the only two in the cafeteria now. "Yes," he said. "I saw him this morning. It's nothing to be concerned about."

Mr. Lupine wouldn't look me in the eye. His upper lip was beaded with sweat. He was definitely hiding something. He pretended to adjust the height of the microphone.

"I saw an animal last night near our teepee village," I said cagily. "It was big. It wasn't like any animal I've ever seen before. It came around in the middle of the night."

Mr. Lupine's hands stopped fidgeting with the microphone. "Well we *are* in the woods," he said, laughing nervously. "There's plenty of wildlife out here. I'm sure it was nothing to worry about." He looked me in the eye suddenly. "You really shouldn't leave your teepee in the middle of the night," he said. "I want you to promise me you'll stay inside from now on, and make sure your door is shut."

I didn't answer. I wasn't sure how much to tell him, but I had to find out what was going on. "I also noticed that the teepee village next to mine is empty now," I said. "Last night it was full of girls."

Mr. Lupine glanced around again. "I'm sure you're mistaken," he said. "I believe the village next to yours has always been empty."

He was lying. I knew he was lying. "But I saw them last night," I said. "And this morning the fire was still warm."

Mr. Lupine laughed nervously. "Oh *that* village," he said. "A couple of the counselors had to leave for a family emergency. We assigned their campers to other villages. That village *is* empty. It slipped my mind."

I'd looked all day for Kristen Faulder. She hadn't been assigned to another teepee village. She was gone. I watched Mr. Lupine's broad and twitching face. My heart was pounding now.

Mr. Lupine is in on it, I thought. He *knows* about his brother. He *knows* what happened to all those vanished campers. I wanted to run out the door. I wanted to run out of the camp. I wanted to run all the way back home.

"I'm sorry to have taken up your time," I croaked. "I think I'll be going now." I turned and started walking toward the cafeteria door, trying hard not to break into a sprint.

"Derek," Mr. Lupine called. I stopped and turned to look at him. I tried to look calm—like I didn't suspect a thing. "Please don't mention to anyone about the empty teepee village," he said. "That's just between you and me."

I nodded, plastered an innocent smile on my face and turned away again. I took a few steps toward the door.

"And, Derek," Mr. Lupine called after me again. I turned back to look at him. "Don't go out of your teepee at night," he warned me. "Just stay inside, and keep the door closed."

"Yes, sir," I said. I turned and slipped out the cafeteria door before he could call me back.

I started down the dark trail to the teepee villages. I had my new flashlight tonight, but I was even more terrified. Each time I heard a twig crack or a mouse scurry through the bushes, I stabbed my flashlight's trembling beam at the noise—half expecting to see Slim's face, fanged and covered with fur, glaring back at me.

Chapter 7

As the days passed, I began to settle into Teepee Village Summer Camp—though I never quite relaxed. The camp was OK during the day, but it was hard to sleep at night. I'd lie awake wondering what was going on outside in the moonlight. Sometimes I'd hear the howling in the distance, and my heart would start racing.

I'd always thought that werewolves only came out when there was a full moon, but I'd hear the howling three or four nights a week—and the new full moon wouldn't arrive for a while yet. Every night, it took a long time before I'd get to sleep.

It didn't help that the Awful Andersons came up with a brand new terrifying story every night, which, they insisted, had really happened to them or some relative. Either they were making the stories up, or their family was about the most unfortunate family since the time of Job. Most nights, I was awake so late, I'd sleep in and miss breakfast the next morning.

And I didn't make any friends. Kristen was right; the kids here tended to keep with the other kids in their own teepee villages. After the first few days, everyone seemed to think I was one of the Andersons, and so they were reluctant to have anything to do with me. If I sat at a table in the dining hall, no one would sit within ten yards of me. They seemed to think I was the kind of guy who might hide a beetle in their mashed potatoes or pour salt in their milk when they weren't looking.

But I wasn't like that at all; I was a helpful and obedient kid. I went to church every Sunday. But, like Kristen said, this camp was full of cliques, and regardless of how I felt about it, I was in the Awful Anderson Clique.

For days, I kept looking for Kristen. I kept hoping she'd turn up swimming at the pool or fishing off the dock. I kept hoping she'd show up at my table with her tray at lunch. I wanted to be proved wrong. I wanted to know that all this stuff about werewolves was just in my imagination. Only then could I relax and start enjoying camp.

But Kristen never showed up. She was definitely gone. I asked around—when anyone would talk to me—and none of the girls' teepee villages seemed to have taken in any new girls since the first week of camp. I was convinced that Mr. Lupine wasn't telling the truth about them. Something had happened to them, and it wasn't what Mr. Lupine claimed.

As I spent more time with the Awful Andersons, I began to realize that they weren't so awful after all. Sometimes I'd go along with them when they went swimming or fishing, and if they started getting out of control, I'd make some excuse and slip away.

The more I hung out with them, the more I liked them. They weren't really mean; they were just rambunctious kids who didn't know what to do with all their energy and didn't know when to stop.

I'm sure they weren't A students, but they had quick minds, and they seemed to all be on one wavelength. They had a habit of talking all at once and finishing each other's sentences.

And they were curious. They were always trying to invent something or learn something new. Could a freshwater trout live in the swimming pool? There was only one way to find out. They caught a two-pound trout, carried it in a pail of water over to the swimming pool and dumped it in. It never occurred to them to ask permission from anybody—and it never occurred to them that all the girls would run squealing from the pool when they were joined by a fish. After all, the same girls swam in the lake all the time, and the lake was full of fish.

Could a wooden picnic table be used as a raft? Once again, there was only one way to know for sure. The Andersons found a perfectly good table outside the archery shed and carried it to the lake. They tossed it off the end of the dock, and jumped on board. It sank, of course, and they swam to shore, soaking wet, but full of new knowledge.

I tried to stay away from them when it looked like they were headed for trouble, and a few times I informed an adult when I heard them contemplating something particularly atrocious. Otherwise, we got along fine.

I started eating my meals with them, since no one else seemed willing to be at the same table with me. But I never got used to the scary stories they told around the campfire.

My second week at camp, the Andersons invited me on one of their "Canoe Conquest" games.

"The most we've got in one hour is seven," Ryan told me. "Everyone paddles away when they see us coming now. I think we'd have a much better chance if we had another hand on deck. What do you say, Dennis?"

I shook my head. "I don't know, guys," I said. "I think I'll just spend some time on my own today. I've got some thinking to do. And my name's Derek."

"Suit yourself," Ryan said.

At lunch that day, someone set a big bowl of apples out on the dessert counter, so I slipped one into my jacket pocket. I thought I'd go out to the lake and find a nice quiet spot where I could be on my own. I went to my teepee and got my Bible and headed out to the shore.

I hiked along the edge of the water for a while. At first, I saw a lot of kids fishing and swimming. But the farther I hiked, the fewer people I saw. When I stopped seeing other kids, I climbed up on a sunny rock that overlooked a little cove. I bit into my apple.

I was lonely up here at camp, and I was anxious. I wasn't sure what to think of all that I'd seen. I'd never been so confused and scared. I thought again about the verse in Deuteronomy: "I will never leave you nor forsake you," and that made me feel a little better. I might not have any kids to play with, but I still had a friend to talk to. I sat praying a while, asking God to help me figure out what was going on. I also asked him to help me feel less lonely.

Suddenly, I heard splashing. I opened my eyes and looked out on the lake to see a canoe full of girls, all in orange life jackets, frantically paddling in the direction of the dock. Behind them another canoe was in fast pursuit. I squinted. Three boys were in the second boat—the Awful Andersons, of course—and they were pelting the girls with what appeared to be apple cores salvaged from the lunch bins.

"Avast, ye maties," Ryan's voice carried across the water. "They be making their escape."

"Fire at will," Nic shouted. "All free hands, fire at will."

"*Cool,*" someone said. That had to be Nathan.

An apple core splashed into the lake, just inches from the girls' canoe, and someone squealed. Though all four girls paddled wildly, the Awful Andersons were gaining on them.

In a few minutes, both canoes were out of sight beyond the cove, though I could still hear pirate talk and the splashing of paddles. A moment later, I heard a loud splash, and girls squealing. Chalk one up for my roommates. No wonder no one would talk to me.

Just then, I noticed someone swimming toward the shore. Actually, the person wasn't really swimming—it was more like a frantic dog paddle. Had one of the girls gotten separated from the canoe? She seemed to be struggling hard to keep her head above water.

I was about to jump off the rock and run down to the shore to see if I could help, when I realized it wasn't a girl at all. It was *Slim,* and he was thrashing through the water with his head sticking up above the surface. I slid down behind the rock so I could watch him without being seen.

In a minute or two, he staggered up on the shore. His bony body was dripping wet. His baggy blue swimming trunks seemed six sizes too big for him. As soon as he set foot on dry land, he shook his head wildly—water flying everywhere. He had no towel, but he didn't appear to need one. His shoulders shook next, and then the shaking seemed to move down his skinny body past his hips to his legs. It was the weirdest thing I'd ever seen. Something was definitely wrong with that man.

That night, the Andersons and I sat around the campfire. It came time for a Terrifying Teepee

Tale. I sat on a log, fidgeting, trying to prepare myself for another scary story. I could hear Slim snoring in his teepee. The fire roared and crackled. Each night the fire seemed bigger, but I didn't dare ask where they were getting all the firewood.

"How come Darryl never tells a story?" Nic asked.

All the others looked at me, their faces lit up orange in the firelight.

I shrugged. "I don't really know any spooky stories," I told them. "And my name's Derek."

"You don't know any stories?" Ryan said.

"Not scary ones."

"What kind, then?"

"Well, I know a lot of Bible stories," I said. "But they're not very scary."

"Any monsters in the Bible?"

I mulled it over. "I guess you could call some of them monsters," I said. "There's Jonah and the big fish, and there's one about a giant called Goliath."

"I think I heard that one," Nic said, nodding. "He had a blue ox or something."

I shook my head. "You're thinking of Paul Bunyan," I told him over the roar of the fire. "That's not actually in the Bible."

"I have a story that's a lot scarier than some guy's bunions," Ryan said.

I laughed. "No," I said. "It's Paul Bunyan—not *Paul's bunions*."

"Whatever," Ryan said. "It's not as scary as the story *I'm* about to tell. And this one really happened."

I might have guessed. I leaned away from the hot fire and tried to get comfortable on the log.

"It was a dark and stormy night," Ryan began, staring into the fire.

"It's *always* a dark and stormy night," Nic pointed out.

"Of course it is," Ryan said. "That's when everything scary happens."

"Not dentist visits," Nic reasoned. "Not math tests."

"OK, *most* scary things happen on a dark and stormy night," Ryan said, obviously annoyed by his cousin's interruptions.

"OK then."

"Well, as I was saying," Ryan continued. "It was a very dark and stormy night. Even darker and stormier than it was in last night's story."

"*Cool,*" Nathan said.

"Anyway, this happened one night when I was a little kid, and our next door neighbor, Muriel, was baby-sitting us. We had a roaring fire going in the fireplace."

"We didn't have a fireplace when we lived next door to Muriel," Nathan interrupted. "Remember that house?"

"OK," Ryan said, even more annoyed. "We had a big space heater in the living room, remember?"

"Sort of."

"OK, well then that was roaring,"

"Sure," Nathan said, nodding. "I remember."

"Anyway, at about eight o'clock the phone rang, and I answered it. No one spoke on the other end, so I just kept saying hello. I was just about to hang up the phone when I heard this evil laugh on the other end—a real deep voice and a really creepy laugh." Ryan burst out with an evil cackle that made me jump a little. "And then the phone went dead."

"*Cool,*" Nathan said again.

"So I told Muriel the baby-sitter, and she said it was probably just some kind of wrong number. And we went back to playing Monopoly. Meanwhile, the storm kept getting worse. And then at nine o'clock the phone rang again, so I picked it up and said hello. A deep voice on the other end said, '*I'm on my way.*' And then that creepy laugh started again. I just about wet my pants and slammed the phone down on its cradle."

"So what did you do?" Nic wanted to know. He was leaning forward, and his eyes were wide.

"I told Muriel, the baby-sitter, and she said it was just some kind of prank. She said it was probably her boyfriend, Scooter, playing a joke on us."

"I remember Scooter," Nathan said. "He was pretty cool. But I don't remember any of this happening."

"You were just a baby," Ryan told him. "Anyway, we called Scooter's house, but Scooter's mom said he was sitting next to her watching TV, and that he definitely hadn't made any phone calls."

Ryan paused and looked us each in the eye before he went on with his story.

"We were supposed to go to bed at nine o'clock," Ryan started up again. "But Muriel was kind of spooked by the phone calls, so she let us stay up late, and we turned on the television and all the lights. Then, at ten o'clock, the phone rang again. I picked up the phone, and Muriel picked up the kitchen extension so she could listen in.

"'Hello?' I said. 'Hello?' My voice was kind of squeaky on account of I was nervous.

"'*I'm getting closer,*' the deep voice said. '*I'll be there by midnight, and then you'll all be dead.*'"

I squirmed a bit and leaned farther away from the fire. Ryan looked at me and smiled.

"Muriel screamed and dropped the phone," Ryan continued. "I hung up my extension and tried to calm her down. She picked up the poker from the fireplace."

"We didn't have a fireplace," Nathan reminded him.

"She picked up my aluminum baseball bat," Ryan went on, as if there had been no interruption. "And we went through the entire house making sure all the doors and windows were locked. There was one high window in the back of the house that had a broken latch, but all the others we locked. And then we went into the living room and tried to watch television. But as it got close to eleven, Muriel and I just stared at the phone, waiting."

"What about me?" Nathan interrupted.

"You were just a baby—and you were kind of stupid anyway—so you didn't know what was going on. You'd fallen asleep on the sofa."

"Maybe I was just brave," Nic said.

"Yeah, *right*," Ryan said. "Whatever. Anyway, at eleven o'clock the phone rang again. I picked it up. *'I'll be there any minute,'* the deep voice said. *'And at midnight you'll all be dead.'* And then that creepy laugh again. I hung up the phone, and as soon as I did, there was a huge flash of lightning. Muriel screamed and started crying. The lights all flickered and then the house plunged into darkness. The electricity was gone. The television was dead.

"Muriel started freaking out. 'He's going to kill us,' she kept screaming. 'We're all going to die.' Then I remembered that the phones still work when the electricity goes out, so I picked up the phone and dialed 9–1–1. A woman answered the phone. I told her everything that had happened. 'It's probably just some kid playing a prank,' she told me.

"'Send over a police car anyway,' I begged her.

"'I can't do that,' she told me. 'There's a big emergency tonight. A crazy killer escaped from the lunatic asylum. All the police are setting up roadblocks and stuff. There's no one available.'"

"You mean the guy with the hook escaped again?" Nathan wanted to know.

"No," Ryan told him. "This was a different guy, and he was even crazier. 'Isn't there anything you can do?' I asked the 9–1–1 lady. 'Our lives may be in danger.' She told me she'd keep monitoring my number, and if anyone called it in the next hour, she'd trace the number and tell us where it was coming from."

Ryan paused. I think I was actually shaking on my log by this time.

"We lit some candles and huddled in the darkness, waiting," Ryan continued slowly. "My wristwatch said eleven thirty, then a quarter to twelve. As soon as the minute hand hit midnight, the phone rang.

"With tingling fingers, I picked the phone up and put it to my ear. *'It's time,'* the deep voice said. *'Prepare to die.'* There was the evil laugh again, and a huge flash of lightning. I hung up the phone. Thunder rumbled across the sky."

The fire suddenly spat a cloud of sparks into the air, and I nearly had a heart attack.

"The phone rang again," Ryan said dramatically. "I snatched it up. It was the woman from 9–1–1. *'Hurry,'* she said. *'Get out of the house! Get out now!'* I asked her why. *'Because the call is coming from your upstairs extension.'"*

There was a long pause. It was the end of the story. I was goose bumps all over.

"So what happened?" Nic asked.

"Duh," Ryan said. "We ran outside, and the police came and caught the crazy guy. He was the one they'd been looking for. They carted him away in a straitjacket."

"Did he have a hook?" Nathan wanted to know.

"No, stupid. Not every crazy guy has a hook," Ryan said. "He *did* have a big scar down his face, but I chose not to mention that since it has nothing to do with the story." Ryan sat back, folded his arms, and looked around at us, as if he expected applause.

"*Cool,*" Nathan said.

"I see one flaw in your story," Nic said.

"Yeah? What's that?"

"You can't call your own number from one of your extensions."

Ryan thought a moment. "Sure you can," he said. "But you have to dial a bunch of special numbers first."

Nic nodded, accepting Ryan at his word.

"I see another flaw with your story," Nathan said.

"What's that?"

"We didn't have an upstairs in that house."

"OK, I forgot. The killer was in the basement."

"We didn't have a basement either."

"Shut up, Nathan."

That was the end of story time for the night. We sat and watched the fire a while, and then Ryan said it was time to turn in.

Chapter 8

I rolled over and sat up on my bunk. I felt all twisted and hot in my sleeping bag. I'd been having a bad dream—I knew that much—but now that I was awake, I couldn't remember what the dream was about. I unzipped the sleeping bag and was pulling out my legs when I heard the noise.

I pulled myself up on my knees and looked out the window. The moon seemed tangled among the black tree branches. No crickets were chirping. I held my breath and listened.

In a moment, the sound came again—the same mournful, throaty howl deep among the trees. I looked at the moon—it wasn't quite full yet. Whatever the sound was, it immediately raised goose bumps on my arms and pricked at the hairs on the back of my neck.

The sound seemed to be deep in the woods tonight, far off among the trees. I knew this was my chance. I knew what I had to do. I had to go see if Slim was in his cabin. If he was there, I could stop worrying. If he was there, I'd know he wasn't a werewolf. If he was there, I'd know I was letting my imagination run away with me.

I didn't really want to go outside—I remembered Mr. Lupine's warning to stay inside at night with the door closed. But if I was ever going to put this thing to rest, I had to see for myself that Slim was snoring in his own teepee, and not out howling at the moon.

I slipped down off my bunk without waking any of the Andersons. I pulled on my jeans and a sweatshirt. I tied on my shoes. I opened the door and then quietly closed it behind me. I pulled back the teepee flap. A ground fog had crept into the village while I'd slept. It had spilled over the fire pit, making it completely invisible, and the mist seemed to climb the sides of each teepee.

I paused in the doorway and listened. I wanted to make sure the howling was still far away before I left the safety of the tent. In a few seconds, the howling began again. This time in a different place—far off to the left, deep among the trees. It was far enough away, I judged. I could make it safely to Slim's teepee and back again.

I took a deep breath and tried to steady my nerves. I slipped out of the doorway and waded through the knee-high fog toward Slim's cabin. I had to be careful not to get too close to the fire pit and twist my ankle on one of the stones around the edge or bang my knee on one of the log benches, so I veered well out of the way. I slipped past the two empty teepees. I found my footing carefully, while the thick mist washed around my legs.

I crept up to Slim's teepee and quietly pulled back the flap. The door was wide open. I froze and listened for Slim's snore. The teepee was silent. Nothing stirred. In the distance, I heard the howl again, but it was hard to know which direction it came from.

I pulled my flashlight from my pocket and switched it on. I shone its bright beam into the cabin from the doorway. I didn't care if I woke Slim up. If I saw him there in bed, at least I'd know he wasn't a werewolf.

But Slim *wasn't* there. The sheets on his bed were twisted and rumpled, like someone had been thrashing around on the bed. I pointed the light around the room. Nothing moved. One of the chairs at his table was lying on the floor on its back, and books and clothes were strewn about on the floor. It looked like someone had ransacked his room.

I stood in the doorway a moment trying to catch my breath. Just then, I heard the howl again, and it made my blood run cold. It was much closer now, and instead of being on the left side of camp like before, now it was on the right. Whatever was out there was moving fast. I switched off my flashlight and poked my head out Slim's teepee flap.

It was settled. It all made sense. Slim was the one out there howling, and now he was on his way back to the teepee village. My first impulse was to dive back into Slim's teepee and hide. But I couldn't let him find me there, and I figured he'd sniff me out pretty easily.

The howl came again, much closer now. I'd have to make a run for it. I'd have to get back to my own teepee as quickly as possible. My heart hammered in my chest. My fingers tingled. I took a deep breath and darted out of the teepee into the mist. I was running now, but I was worried about tripping over something in the fog. I zigzagged this way and that, dodging the places where I thought the log benches might be. The howling seemed closer now. It seemed to be right out among the closest trees.

I made it past the fire pit and dashed toward my teepee. I ripped open the flap and dove inside. I pushed the door open, ducked inside and slammed it behind me, not caring if I woke the Andersons. I was thrilled to be back inside my own teepee. I stood in the pitch-black darkness, grinning and catching my breath. I was safe.

And then I heard it. The unmistakable sound of paws pounding the ground outside. The werewolf was in the teepee village now. I heard panting and growling. Part of me wanted to peek outside, but I didn't dare.

And then I heard a new sound. A sniffing. It grew louder and louder, like it was following the trail of my scent from Slim's teepee to my own.

I threw my body against the door and felt in the dark for the brass bolt that would lock it. I ran my hand up and down the rough doorframe, but I couldn't find it. My eyes were adjusting to the darkness now.

I'm not sure if it was the musty smell or the heavy silence of the place, but something didn't seem right. A sickening thought occurred to me. I reached up with my hand and touched the gauze-like layer of cobwebs above my head. *I was in the wrong teepee!* I was in the empty teepee full of tiny paw prints!

I reached into my pocket and fumbled with my flashlight. Something small scampered across the wooden floor in the darkness. The sound made my stomach lurch. I *hate* rats! In my haste, I dropped my flashlight and heard it roll away from me across the wooden floor.

I couldn't move. There was no lock on the door, and I had to hold it shut. My heart was in my throat. I felt light-headed. Something tiny scurried past behind me. I thought I felt it brush against the heels of my tennis shoes. I had to get out of this teepee! My skin crawled. I felt like I was suffocating.

I was about to pull the door open and make a run for it when something outside threw its heavy body against the door. I heard a frantic sniffing and scratching and growling. I flattened my body against the door.

There were a few seconds of silence. Enough time for me to begin worrying about the creatures inside the teepee again. Then I heard something brush against the canvas sides of the teepee. The sound wasn't inside. It was out there! First it was to my left, and then it was on my right. The werewolf was circling the teepee, trying to find another way in! Another rat scampered across the dusty wooden floor. I felt like I was going to faint. I couldn't take this anymore.

I closed my eyes and prayed that God would get me out of here. When I opened my eyes again, everything was silent. I held my breath and listened. There was no sound outside. Had the creature gone back into the woods? Had it gone back into Slim's teepee to become a human again? In the silence, I could hear my own heart beating.

And then I heard a new sound—crickets chirping!

I pulled the door open a crack and peeked out. The teepee flap was wide open. I could see the low fog, silver in the moonlight. The ground right in front of me was all torn up.

I pulled the door open wide and slipped over to the teepee flap. I peeked outside. The moonlight shone through the treetops and lit the teepee village with an eerie silver light. The mist crept along the ground like a heavy, slow-moving river. I listened.

I stood there feeling the damp breeze move through my hair, barely daring to breathe. No other sound came, only the constant chirping of the crickets. There was no movement except the slow creeping mist. I waited. I stood there for what seemed like hours, not daring to move.

It's gone away, I told myself. *It's miles away by now. It's definitely safe to go back to your teepee. The crickets are chirping.*

But I didn't move. I just stood there, frozen with fear.

It took me a while. I deliberated and argued with myself. *You're being a big baby*, I told myself. *There's nothing to be afraid of.*

I must have waited another twenty minutes before I dared to move. I took a couple of hesitant steps out of the teepee on wobbly legs. Nothing moved.

I took another step. The ground fog washed around me like a restless, silent ocean.

I took another step, and a twig snapped underfoot.

And then I heard it—a low, throaty growl as deep and resonant as a bear's. It came from the direction of Slim's teepee. I froze. In the shadows of Slim's doorway I saw two cold eyes glimmer in the moonlight.

The growl came again, menacing and deep. And then the mist swirled, as a huge dark shape galloped out of the doorway toward me.

I sprinted for my teepee, stumbling across the uneven ground. Paws clawed the earth behind me. I ducked inside the flap and pushed the door open. I jumped inside and slammed the door behind me.

I was reaching for the lock when the door jolted open a little. I pushed against it with all my might to keep it closed. I felt a cold, wet nose press through the crack before the creature yelped and pulled back. The door slammed shut, but the creature snarled and scratched. I slid the lock into place and stepped back, trembling.

It was suddenly silent outside. All I could hear was the Andersons snoring—they'd slept through the entire ordeal! I pulled the chain that turned on the light. Ryan rolled over but kept snoring. The other two didn't even stir.

I wanted to wake them all up. I wanted company. I wanted to tell them everything that had happened. But what would be the point? No one would ever believe me—not even the Andersons. They'd think it was just another campfire tale.

In a few seconds, the crickets took up their chirping again. It was over. I was safe inside. I said a prayer of thanks and pulled the chain. The light went out.

When I woke up, the teepee was hot. The Andersons were gone. It must have been nearly noon. I got dressed and went outside.

In the bright sunlight, the teepee village looked much as it always had, except for some scratches on the empty teepee's door, and a few spots of earth that were torn up. Now that the sun was out, it was hard to believe what had happened the night before. Had I dreamed the whole thing?

I crept near Slim's teepee and heard him snoring inside. I suppose it was possible that the whole thing was a dream. I walked around the village, looking at the ground for animal tracks, but the earth there was pretty hard, and I couldn't find anything definite.

I walked behind the empty teepee where I'd hidden. There was a little patch of soft soil back there, and it had been trampled with countless paw prints. A narrow trail led into the woods. It was barely visible—not a human trail, more like something an animal might make. It was mostly just trampled-down grass. I took a few steps along it. I had to turn sideways and raise my hands above my head to get through. I found another patch of sandy earth. It held a neat row of perfect paw prints leading away from the teepee village.

I wasn't sure what to do. I didn't want to wander off into the woods for fear of getting lost. But I knew Slim was snoring in his teepee, and I wanted to find out what was going on. I followed the trail a few more yards, trying to keep track of the paw prints. The marks would disappear at a patch of rocky ground, and I'd have to search around in the bushes and under the trees to find where they picked up again.

I kept looking back to maintain my bearings. I didn't want to go so far that I couldn't see the tips of the teepees in the distance. As long as I could see camp, I knew I could get back.

Even though it was daylight and I knew Slim was back at camp, I was a little jumpy. Every time a twig snapped underfoot or a squirrel scrambled through the underbrush, my heart would take off racing.

Eventually, I lost track of the footprints. I hunted all through the bushes for a broken twig or pressed-down grass, anything that would let me know which way the creature had gone. I was just about to turn around and head back to my teepee—I could just barely distinguish the distant pointed tops of the tents from all the pointed pine trees—when I saw a patch of sand and three clear paw prints crossing it.

I looked down at the big paw prints. I glanced back in the direction of camp. I knew I should go no further. I looked down the path where the tracks seemed to lead, and then I saw it. It was dangling from a bush, a bright orange scrap of cloth. I went over and tugged it loose from the bush. It was a hat with earflaps. I turned it over. It was torn and covered with dried mud. The visor was missing and one of the earflaps looked like it had been gnawed upon.

I dropped the hat and ran back through the thick woods toward the distant teepee village, my heart pounding in my chest.

Chapter 9

The rest of the day, I walked around in a daze. I don't remember eating lunch or dinner. I don't remember a single thing I did. I felt burdened with a terrible knowledge, and the knot in my stomach seemed to twist tighter and tighter inside me.

There was a werewolf on the loose out there! Was I the only camper who knew about it? Who could I tell? Who could I trust? Mr. Lupine was probably in on it, and most of the rest of the staff were members of his family. Who knows how many of them also knew Slim's secret! For all I knew, every counselor, janitor, and kitchen helper was in on it.

The worst part was I knew no one would believe me. They'd think I was just one of the

Awful Andersons. They'd think I was the kind of kid who sits around the campfire telling tall tales and pretending they're true. And this was just about the tallest tale they were likely to hear.

I wasn't sure about the Awful Andersons. I figured they'd believe me—they seemed to believe everything they heard. But what might the Awful Andersons do if they thought there was a werewolf loose in the camp? They were out of control as it was. I shuddered to imagine what kind of stunt they'd pull if they thought they were really in danger.

I was confused and tangled up in my own thoughts. Part of me was ready to call 9–1–1. Another part thought I had lost my mind. How could any of this be true? Yet, what other explanation was there for everything I'd seen?

At the last full moon, an entire teepee village of kids had vanished. From what I could tell, tonight would be a full moon too. Was it going to be *our* turn this time? If I was going to do something, I had to make my mind up fast.

I sat on a log at the campfire that night with the flames roaring in front of me. The full moon hung high in the sky. I glanced over my shoulder at Slim's tent. I could hear him in there snoring.

As long as he was snoring, I guessed we were safe. As long as Slim was snoring, everything was all right. I just hoped he'd snore all night and prove me wrong.

"It's time for another Terrifying Teepee Tale," Ryan said suddenly.

His announcement didn't bother me much tonight. My real life was much scarier than any story the Andersons were likely to tell. In fact, a good story might be just the distraction I needed.

"Who's got one tonight?"

"When are *you* going to tell a story, Daniel?" Ryan wanted to know.

"Like I said, I don't know any," I told him. I didn't even bother reminding him that my name was Derek.

"Well then make one up," he said.

"Why don't one of you guys tell one?" I said. "I just feel like listening tonight."

"*I've* got a story," Nathan said.

"Hit it, maestro," Ryan told him.

"This one's about our Aunt Lydia," Nathan said.

"We don't *have* an Aunt Lydia," Ryan interrupted.

"Not any more we don't," Nathan said. "And this story tells why."

"*Coo-o-o-l,*" Nic said.

"It happened way back in the old days before even Ryan was born," Nathan began. "Aunt Lydia was in high school. She was very pretty, but her family was very poor. All kinds of boys were in love with her, but she never went out with any of them on account of she was embarrassed by how poor her family was—and she didn't want any of the other kids at school to know where she lived.

"Aunt Lydia fell in love with the captain of the football team, but she was too shy to ever talk to him. Every time he came near her, she'd start shaking all over, and she'd have to run away.

"As it got close to graduation, she knew the boy she loved was going off to college on a football scholarship. She'd probably never see him again. She wished she had the courage to talk to him, but she could never get up the nerve.

"Anyway, as the senior prom got nearer, lots of boys began asking Lydia out, on account of she was so pretty. But she turned them all down because she knew she couldn't afford a decent prom dress, and she didn't want anyone to see her house.

"But the week before the prom, the impossible happened. The captain of the football team walked up to her in the cafeteria and asked her to go to the prom with him. He told her that he'd always wanted to ask her out, but that she always seemed to run away from him, and he was afraid she didn't like him.

"Of course Aunt Lydia said yes, but then she had a big problem. Her family couldn't afford to buy her a pretty dress, and there wasn't enough time to get a job to earn the money.

"She thought that maybe she could find a nice outfit in a thrift shop somewhere. And maybe she could fix it up and get a decent looking dress for hardly any money. She looked in the phone book for thrift shops and second-hand clothing stores, and she found an ad for a place that sold second-hand formal wear for all ages. It said they had suits and dresses and shoes, and that everything was under ten dollars.

"Aunt Lydia couldn't believe her luck. She got the phone and dialed the number, hoping the ad wasn't a misprint. This guy answered the phone and gave her the address of the store. He told her to hurry over because he had to get started at his second job as soon as it got dark.

"Aunt Lydia took all the money she had in the world and caught a bus to the other side of town. She found the address, but instead of being a store, it was somebody's house. She went up and knocked on the door, and this creepy pale guy answered the door. He had dark lines under his eyes, like he hadn't had much sleep lately.

"'Is this the place that sells second-hand formal wear?' Aunt Lydia asked.

"'Yes, it is,' the man told her. 'Come on in and I'll show you what I've got. And if you don't see anything you like, I get new stuff in every day.'

"He took her to a room that was full of clothing racks. It had kind of a weird smell, but there were hundreds of dark suits and beautiful dresses, and there were piles of shoes. Most of the clothes looked like the styles old people wear, but there were some nice dresses too.

"She picked out a really nice dress and a pair of shoes, and they only cost her fifteen dollars instead of a couple hundred. And they looked brand new, like no one had ever worn them before. She bought the clothes and headed back home on the bus.

"When the night came for the prom, Aunt Lydia looked beautiful in her new white dress. She took the bus to the school, since she'd promised to meet the football captain there, but along the way she started to feel a little woozy.

"When she got off the bus, she was pretty dizzy. She stumbled to the school and managed to climb the front steps, determined to meet her handsome date for the evening. She managed to make it to the gym where the prom was being held. Everyone stopped to watch her as she staggered toward the football captain. She collapsed unconscious into his arms. A few minutes later, she was dead.

"The autopsy showed that she had died from being poisoned with embalming fluid. They tested the dress and found that it was full of all kinds of toxic chemicals. It turned out that the man who sold her the dress was a grave robber, and he tried to make extra money by selling the clothes his victims were buried in."

It was just about the sickest story I'd ever heard, even though I knew it wasn't true.

"That's not a true story," Nic objected.

"Yeah, it is," Ryan said. "I bought a nice pair of pants from the guy once." The three of them started laughing.

"Hey, the fire's going out," Nathan said.

I had no idea what he was talking about. The flames were at least six feet in the air.

"Better go get more wood," Ryan said.

"Hey, Dylan," Nathan said to me. "You think I can borrow your flashlight a minute?"

"My name's Derek," I said. "And I lost my flashlight. I haven't seen it all day."

"Maybe you dropped it last night," a voice behind me said. I just about jumped into the fire. I spun around. Slim was standing behind me, his gaunt face flickering in the firelight. "Maybe you left it in the empty teepee," he said. A yellow, flickering smile spread across his face.

How did he know? No one saw me go into the other teepee last night—*no one human, anyway.*

"Well, I can't sleep," Slim said. "Think I'll go for a walk." He trudged over toward the trail to the main camp. But instead of heading down the trail, he disappeared into the dark woods. It took a few minutes for me to catch my breath. I was convinced now. Slim was *definitely* a werewolf.

And tonight was a full moon!

Nathan stumbled back into the circle of light made by the fire, his arms loaded down with firewood. He dumped a few more logs in the fire pit, and the fire spat a cloud of sparks skyward. I barely noticed.

I cleared my throat. "I believe it's *my* turn to tell a story," I said. Everyone fell silent and looked at me.

"It's about time," Ryan said.

I looked around the fire at them. They were all smiling at me. I could tell they weren't expecting much. They were just glad to see me joining in at last.

I looked into the fire and took a deep breath. "This is a true story," I said.

"*All* our stories are true," Ryan objected.

"Yeah," I said. "But mine *really* happened."

"Oh," Ryan said. "*That* kind of true."

It was hard to know where to begin. I decided to just plunge in and hope it would all turn out OK. "This is about the time my Mom dropped me off at Teepee Village Summer Camp," I said.

I started at the beginning and told them everything I knew about Slim: the color-blindness, the raw meat, the bruise, the howling, the missing campers, the full moon, the orange hat with the ear flaps. It was quite a catalogue of evidence.

When I was finished I looked up from the fire. No one said anything for a while. We all just stared into the fire.

"*Coo-o-o-l,*" Nathan said.

"Dude, you're good," Nic said.

"You guys, he's *serious,*" Ryan told them, wide eyed. "Slim's *really* a werewolf."

Nic and Nathan fell silent a moment, considering the news.

"*Nah,*" said Nic. "You're pulling my leg. That stuff didn't really happen."

"It did," I told him. "Every word was true."

Nathan and Nic fell silent again. They were quiet for a long time.

"No wonder the guy chases cats," was all Nic could think of to say.

A mournful howl sounded in the forest suddenly, in the same direction were Slim had disappeared a few minutes earlier. Like it was some kind of cue, we all looked up at the big yellow moon above us. Nic and Nathan bolted for the teepee. Ryan and I were right on their heels.

By the time we reached the teepee, though, the door was already locked. Ryan hammered on the door with his fist. "Let us in, you idiots," he yelled.

"Are you alone?" Nic wanted to know.

"Of course we're alone," Ryan said. Another howl sounded in the woods, this time from the opposite side of camp. Ryan pounded on the door again. *"Open up!"*

The door swung open, and we scrambled inside. Nathan slipped the lock back in place.

We sat in the darkness listening to Slim's howling as he moved through the woods. It never occurred to any of us that we could just reach up and turn on the light.

"Gee, R-R-Ryan," Nic stammered. "He ate a whole village full of girls last time. You think we're on the menu tonight?"

It sounded pretty silly when someone said it right out loud.

"There had to be two dozen girls and four counselors over there," Nathan said. "He's got quite an appetite."

The howl sounded from the woods behind our teepee, and it was immediately answered by another howl, way off to the right.

"You hear that?" I said. "There's more than one of them!"

"*That's* how all those girls disappeared," Ryan said breathlessly. "The woods are probably crawling with werewolves."

"Maybe being a werewolf is genetic," Nic said. "Practically everyone who works at this camp is related. Mr. Lupine is color-blind too, remember?"

That idea had never occurred to me—but as if to affirm it, three howls came all at once from three different directions. A chill went through me.

"We've got to make a run for it," Nic said in a panic. "We've got to get out of here."

"Where are we going to hide?" Nathan sputtered. "Slim probably knows these woods like the back of his paw. We're all going to die."

"What we need are some silver bullets," Nic said, like we might find some in the teepee if we just looked really hard. "Silver bullets are the only way to kill a werewolf."

"No, I think that's how you kill the Lone Ranger," Nathan told him. "Werewolves have something to do with wooden stakes."

By now the howls were continuous and on all sides of us. I sat in the darkness shivering.

"You know," Nathan said, quietly. "I love *telling* scary stories, but I hate being *in* one."

"What do you think will happen?" Nic asked no one in particular. "You think the lock on the door will hold?"

"It did last night," I told him.

"But what if one of them gets in?" Nathan said.

"The Lord will protect us," I told them. I thought of the words from Deuteronomy again. "'Be strong and courageous,'" I quoted. "'Do not be afraid or terrified because of them, for the Lord your God goes with you; He will never leave you nor forsake you.'"

Everyone was suddenly silent. I knew they were all listening to me. "How about I tell you a story from the Bible?" I said.

"Is it scary?" Nic wanted to know. "I'm not really in the mood for a scary story at this point."

"It's not really scary," I reassured him. "It's about how one little boy went up against a monster with God's help."

I told the Andersons the whole story of David and Goliath—the giant's armor, the five smooth stones, David's assurance that God would go with him.

I couldn't believe it. They sat and listened. They hung on my every word. Was it possible they'd never heard the story before? When I got to the part where David's stone struck Goliath on the forehead, the boys cheered.

When I was done, we all sat silently in the dark. The howling outside continued, and we were all still petrified—but somehow I think we felt braver.

"Slim knows where we are," Nathan said. "He knows right where to find us. You think that lock's strong enough to keep a whole pack of werewolves out?"

"I think so," Ryan said. "That's a good solid door. I think we'll be all right."

I listened to the howling in the woods outside. It was a spooky mournful chorus now—at least four or five voices weaving in and out.

"Ryan's right," Nic said. "They won't be able to get in here, so they'll just go eat one of the other villages."

I suddenly felt sick. All this time I'd never thought of the other villages—I'd just been thinking of myself. On the last full moon, I'd scared Slim away from our camp with a rock—and all the girls in the next village had disappeared. Was that *my* fault? I felt horrible. I couldn't let that happen again.

"We've got to warn the other kids," I said. "They're all sitting ducks. They have no idea what's going on."

"He's right," Ryan said. "But how can we warn them?"

"The wolves haven't attacked yet," I said. "Maybe we've got time to run through the camp and warn everyone."

"But they'll eat us," Nathan said.

"We've got to trust that God will protect us," I said. "It's the only way to save those kids' lives."

"But they'll eat us," Nathan said again.

"If you don't want to come with us, you can stay here," Ryan told him.

Nathan was silent for a few seconds. The howling continued outside. "I don't think I want to stay here on my own," he said. "And I can run pretty fast."

"If a werewolf starts chasing us, you're not going to outrun it," Nic told him bluntly. "They're much faster than people are."

"If a werewolf starts chasing us, I just have to outrun *you*," Nathan pointed out.

"Stop it, you two," Ryan said. "We've got to do this." He stood up. We all stood up. "We'll be heroes," Ryan said in the darkness. "We'll run through the woods yelling, 'The werewolves are coming! The werewolves are coming!' It'll be like the midnight ride of Paul Bunyan."

I didn't bother to correct him. I just bowed my head and started praying out loud. I prayed that God would protect us. I prayed that He'd protect all the other innocent kids in the camp. I prayed that He'd give us courage, speed, and stamina.

I went over to the door and slid back the bolt.

"You guys ready?" I whispered.

"Yeah."

"Yep."

"Sort of."

I pulled the door open. A ground mist had begun to creep into the camp again. I stepped out into the cold mountain air and looked up at the full moon. I felt the other three fall in behind me.

The howling came from deep in the woods— in all different directions.

"Here goes," I said. "Follow me."

I took off running. I turned down the dark forest trail that led past the other teepee villages. The other three ran behind me. I sprinted across the uneven ground, but my footing was sure. I dashed through the dark woods, but I never lost track of the trail.

We passed the empty teepee village in the moonlight, and I remembered the last full moon, when I'd seen it all lit up and full of girls. That couldn't happen again. We had to warn the other campers. Everything depended on us.

By the time we got to the next teepee village, my side was beginning to hurt. "Lock your doors," I shouted as loud as I could. "The werewolves are coming!" A light went on in one of the teepees.

"Stay inside and lock your doors," Ryan yelled. The others yelled things too. And then the howls came. It was as if they were answering our calls.

There was no time to lose. I ran back to the trail and headed toward the other villages. At each new teepee village, we paused and yelled until a light went on, or someone stuck his head out of a teepee flap. "Stay inside and lock your doors," we'd yell. "The werewolves are coming."

And each time we did, the werewolves answered—their howling slowly closing in on our voices. The ground fog grew thicker the closer we got to the main camp. It was hard to see the trail, but still we ran. We had to warn the last teepee village.

My side ached. My legs felt rubbery. I staggered down the last stretch of trail to the final teepee village. I stumbled into the clearing. "Lock your doors," I gasped between gulps of air. "Lock your doors and stay inside. They're coming." A door flap rustled. I heard the three Andersons come up behind me.

"Lock your doors!" Ryan shouted. "There's a bunch of werewolves coming."

And then I heard it—it was directly ahead of us, maybe twenty yards away, but buried in the mist—a deep throaty growl. It came from right between two of the teepees. I froze.

The growl came again—low and menacing. I heard the three boys behind me take off running.

And then the mist swirled, and a huge dark shape lunged at me. I took off running, screaming, flailing as fast as I could back up the trail we'd just come down.

I heard paws beating the ground behind me. Up ahead I heard the Andersons running and shouting. I remembered what Nathan had said. They didn't have to outrun the werewolf; they just had to outrun me!

I dug down deep inside and pushed myself faster. My lungs felt ready to explode. My head grew dizzy.

Was it my imagination, or was there more than one set of paws pounding down the trail behind me?

The mist swirled up around my armpits now, but I didn't slow down. I couldn't slow down.

Soon I was thrashing through the bushes, dodging the trees. I wasn't on the trail anymore, but I just kept running. Tree branches lashed at my face, twisted roots tried to trip and tangle me, but still I ran—my mind praying frantically, my lungs aching for air.

Suddenly, out of the mist, I saw a tall rickety fence. I scrambled over it and stumbled through the bushes on the other side. I was really lost now. "Guys," I called, as loudly as I dared. "Guys, where are you?"

I got no answer, so I just kept running.

If the fence had stopped the werewolves, it wasn't for long. In a few seconds I could hear their huge bodies, thrashing through the woods on either side of me. I could hear them panting and snuffling as they ran.

I stumbled blindly through the woods, getting scraped and pummeled by the low pine branches. I could see the werewolves' muscular bodies bound through the mist and weave through the trees. They were ahead of me and behind me. They were to my left and to my right.

My head swam. My chest seemed ready to explode. I could run no more.

I stumbled into a small clearing and bent double, trying to catch my breath, feeling like I might throw up. The woods around me grew silent. And then the growling began. They were all around me, and they closed in on me slowly. Their bodies began to take shape in the mist as they got closer.

I backed against the trunk of a tree and prayed hard. "Help me, Lord," I said aloud. "Tell me what I should do."

"Darren. Up here," a voice from the sky said. I looked up. There, silhouetted against the stars, were the Awful Andersons sitting together on a high limb. "Climb up here, dude," Ryan said. "Werewolves can't climb trees."

"That's the theory we're working with, anyway," Nathan said.

I scrambled up the tree faster than I could believe, and in a moment I joined them on the limb. I was scraped, sore, and exhausted—but alive.

Chapter 10

I think I actually dozed off a few times, straddling the branch and hugging the tree's trunk. For a while, I heard the werewolves growling and circling the tree. I'd see the mist stir up when they galloped by beneath us. Their large black domed heads sometimes rose above the fog. They knew we were up here, but they weren't able to climb the tree.

Soon the dawn began to break, and the trees were lit up in the gray light. In my confusion I thought I saw what looked like huge black poodles moving through the last wisps of fog. Then the werewolves were gone. I think I dozed off again. The next thing I knew, it was morning.

"I think I found them," a voice called out below us. I groggily looked around. Ryan, Nathan, and Nic were still sitting on the branch. They must have stayed awake all night.

I looked down at the ground. Slim, Mr. Lupine and several of the camp counselors stood on the ground looking up at us.

"What's wrong with you boys?" Slim called up to us, his hands on his hips. "What are you doing out here?" I tried to think of what to say. I was feeling pretty disoriented.

"We know what you are," Nathan called down at him. "You're a werewolf. Or maybe some other kind of monster—we're not quite sure."

Slim shrugged. "I told you," he said to the small group of camp staff. "They're all nuts."

"Come on down from there," Mr. Lupine told us.

"No way," Ryan said. "You're one of them."

"One of them?" Mr. Lupine said.

"A werewolf," Ryan said. "You can't fool us."

Mr. Lupine looked around at the other staff members and then up at us again. "Is there some kind of medication you boys are supposed to be taking?" he wanted to know.

"Save your breath," Ryan said. "We know what's going on here. We know what happened to all those missing girls."

"Missing girls?" Mr. Lupine said. "You mean the ones who got the chicken pox?"

"Chicken pox?" Ryan said.

"Yeah," Mr. Lupine said. "They were in the next teepee village to yours. We took them to the medical center and called their parents. We didn't want to start a panic. We didn't want everyone pulling their kids out of camp. Those girls were the only ones exposed to it."

"Chicken pox?" Ryan said again.

Mr. Lupine nodded. "What did you *think* happened to them?"

Ryan, Nathan and Nic all looked over at me. I kept my mouth shut.

"What about all the creatures we saw?" Ryan asked. "How do you explain them?"

Mr. Lupine pointed behind us. I twisted to look over my shoulder. About a hundred yards behind us was a large red barn. LUPINE POODLE FARM, a sign on the barn read. Beneath that it read: "Arnold Lupine—Champion Breeder."

"We bought the camp because it was right next door," Mr. Lupine told us. "We needed to diversify. Not too many people want full-size poodles anymore. They just want the toy ones."

"What about Slim?" Ryan said. "Why does Slim keep going out at night?"

"We've been having trouble with the fences around the poodle farm," Mr. Lupine said. "The dogs keep getting loose, and Slim has to round them all up."

Ryan looked at me again. The raw meat, the howling, the midnight trips—just about everything was explained. I just grinned dopily and shrugged my shoulders.

"You guys still haven't explained what you're doing up there," Mr. Lupine pointed out. "Or why you woke up the whole camp last night with your shouting."

Ryan looked at me and then back at Mr. Lupine. "We'd rather not talk about it," Ryan said. "But I think we're ready to come down."

A few days later, camp was over. The four of us mostly stayed in our own teepee village those last few days. It was just too embarrassing. We woke up every camper in the village that night, trying to warn them. And now they knew the whole stupid story.

We just hung around the teepee during the day and around the fire at night. We kind of had a new agreement. When the fire was lit, the Andersons told me scary stories, and I told them Bible stories.

It was a big relief that last Friday to have my sleeping bag and suitcases packed in the back of Mom's station wagon—but to tell the truth I was kind of sad to be leaving the Awful Andersons.

"I'm sorry about the whole poodle thing," I told them. We were all standing in the parking lot. The Andersons' sleeping bags and luggage stood between us on the ground. "It was an honest mistake."

"No sweat," Nathan said. "Next to trapping the skunk, it was the coolest thing that happened to us up here."

I laughed.

"And we've got a great new campfire story," Nic added. "We just need to work on the ending a little."

"And thanks for telling us all that stuff about the Bible," Ryan said. "I especially liked the story about Derek and Goliath."

I laughed. "That's *David* and Goliath," I said. "And hang on a minute."

I opened the back door to the station wagon and rummaged around in my duffel bag until I found what I wanted. I went back to the Andersons. "Here," I said, holding the Bible out to them. "I want you to have this. There are all kinds of cool stories in here."

The Andersons looked at each other.

"Go ahead," I said. "I have another one at home."

Ryan reached out and took the Bible. "Thanks," he said. He looked like he didn't often get gifts from people, and he wasn't sure how to react. "Wow," he said nodding. "Thanks."

I reached across all the luggage between us and shook each of their hands. "You guys have been good friends," I told them. "I'm going to miss you. But I'll see you next year."

"Didn't I tell you?" Mom said as we drove down the mountain. "Didn't I tell you you'd make some friends? Didn't I tell you you'd have the time of your life? I'll bet you have plenty of stories to tell me."

I smiled and looked out the window. Ahead of us, at the base of the mountain I could see the lights of civilization. "I've got one pretty good story," I told her. "But it really needs to be told around a campfire."

Don't Miss another exciting

Heebie Jeebies

adventure!

Turn the page to check out a chapter from

Along Came a Spider

Chapter 1

I've been scared before, but nothing like when we moved. A magnolia tree loomed over our new neighborhood like a dark green cloud, twice the height of the oaks and elms around it. They were tall by normal standards, but the magnolia tree dwarfed them.

I followed my older brother to the roots of the massive trunk. Twenty feet up, the huge branches split in three directions around a weathered tree house. Other platforms and rooms rested on limbs at different points.

"Check out the mag tree," Conner marvelled. "It's like a tree town up there." He wove his fingers together and cracked his knuckles. "We've *got* to climb this one, Sis."

"Now?" I checked my watch. The short hand angled past seven.

Conner scanned the tree from bottom to top. His chin dropped. "Come on, Jaime. What else are we going to do?"

"Go home. Unpack." I had clothes to put away. A closet to organize. So did Conner.

He stepped on a wood rung nailed to the trunk and grabbed another above his head. "Are you coming or not?" Before I could answer, he lifted himself from the ground. The wood boards wrapped around the trunk like a spiral staircase.

"The steps are rotten, Conner," I called up to him. "And it's getting dark."

He ignored me.

I circled the tree, watching my brother. "I'll tell Mom and Dad where I last saw you. And how I tried to warn—"

"Go ahead," he interrupted.

"And how I never saw you again." I paused for my brother's next wisecrack. Conner spoke with his shoes, stepping from one rung to the next. With my neck doubled back, I felt like I was standing beneath the world's largest natural canopy. Limbs, branches, and twigs grew in every direction. The leaves were hand-sized and shiny, like plastic. They numbered in the millions and hid the sky. I wondered if, even on its best day, the sun could penetrate the one-tree forest above me.

"This is awesome!" Conner blurted out. He disappeared into the tree house. Seconds later, his blond head poked through the window. "Come on, Jaime. Check it out."

I crossed my arms. I could see the top story of our house from where I stood. Just thinking about what I *wasn't* getting done made me feel guilty.

"Chicken-n-n-n . . . Chicken-n-n-n," Conner chanted.

I debated. I had nothing against climbing. Or tree houses. Normally, I would have been right behind him. But when I left my old, familiar home, I left my confidence with it. I had too many adjustments to make. A new town (totally creepy). A new house (really ancient). And new friends (if I could make some).

Conner went poultry on me. "Bawk. Bawk-bawk."

"Bawk yourself," I yelled back. I grabbed a board and pulled myself up. In a month, I'd begin high school—with or without friends. Time to get tough. I wasn't the bravest kid on earth, but I wasn't a chicken either. Conner was only two years older than me. If he could climb it, so could I.

"Hurry up," my brother called down.

I picked up the pace. Rusty nails held the slats in place, and the wood felt like it would crumble in my hands. But I kept going. Five feet. Ten. My hair fell in my eyes. I paused to brush it aside, then continued. But I didn't get far.

A speckled brown spider scurried over my hand.

"Gross!" I shrieked, flinging it into the air.

"That's a quarter," Conner shouted. A while ago, my parents got sick and tired of me using the word "gross." They imposed a twenty-five-cent fine for every time I said it. When they caught me, I usually responded by saying "gross" again, which immediately put me deeper in the hole.

"No way. It was a spider. A *spider!*"

"Not a *spider?!*" Conner mocked. "How *gross!*"

"But it was!"

"Sorry, Miss Muffet. You owe."

"Sorry, Miss Muffet, you owe," I mimicked, using my baby voice. My parents overdid it with the "fine" thing. But they definitely had a point. I got my mileage out of "gross." Sometimes I said it with two syllables, as in *ga-ross.* Other times I hissed my esses like a snake. But so did my friends, and they didn't get fined a quarter.

I examined the rungs and trunk before starting again. The tree house was only a few more feet above me. Pretty soon, I climbed through the floor hatch and stood up inside. The main tree house compared in size to a small bedroom, but with a lower ceiling. A scrap of carpet covered the floor.

The walls were gray plywood. No paint. No posters. I did a slow three-sixty, taking note of what owned the corners. Cobwebs.

"Come out here," Conner said.

He didn't have to ask twice. I edged through a door that led to a view deck. A railing secured half of it. The rest was open like a diving platform.

"We'll make this railing our first project," Conner said. He admired the rooms and decks throughout the giant tree. "I can't believe someone would give up on this place."

I couldn't either. It was a tree city all right. Ropes, planks, and ladders connected the rooms, which came in all shapes and sizes. Some had roofs, some had walls, some rails. Some were nothing more than platforms nailed to branches.

"Let's check it out," Conner said. He climbed like an ape up one of the limbs. I watched him for a minute, then went back inside. A fuzzy, gray spider scurried for a crack in the wood. It got there before I could flatten it. I studied the dark crevice, wondering how many other spiders were in there. That's when I noticed that half of the wall had been varnished. Only half.

Weird. Another unfinished detail.

When I returned to the deck, Conner was out of sight. "Conner?"

No answer. I moved with caution along the limb he had taken. My fingernails snagged on the rough bark. I edged higher. Suddenly, a branch moved beneath my hand. I watched in horror as an eight-legged leaf crawled from the spot I was holding. "Gross!" I screamed. I knew from science class that eight legs could only mean one thing. It wasn't a lizard. Or a moth. Or an insect. It was a spider.

I yelled for Conner to help. He didn't answer. He didn't even say anything about me owing another quarter.

"Conner?" I called out. "Are you all right?"

I heard a slap through the dense foliage. Skin against skin.

I searched the dark, upper branches. "Conner, what happened? What's wrong?"

I heard movement far above me. Leaves shaking together. Denim sliding on bark.

"Never mind," Conner finally said.

I wouldn't let up. "It was a spider, wasn't it?"

"It's dead now. Who cares?"

"Did it bite you?"

Conner slid down a rope to the platform I was sitting on. The loose rail made me nervous. One wrong step and I'd be toast. A smear of spider legs and guts painted Conner's neck. So did blood.

"Gro—," I caught myself in time. I stretched his shirt collar to get a better look. "It did bite you, huh?"

"Maybe."

"It's already swollen."

Conner softly touched his neck. "Not much."

"Not yet," I countered. "Let's get out of here."

Conner scanned the far reaches of the tree, lingering over the half-finished rooms and decks. I could tell he didn't want to leave. "Stupid spider."

"Come on," I told him. I started down. "Stay above me. If you pass out, I'll catch you."

"Pass out? Sure." Conner laid on the tough-guy attitude. But when he touched his neck, he winced.

We carefully worked our way down, avoiding spiders and webs all the way. It seemed the number of them had doubled since we first climbed the tree. I figured we were home free when we reached the main tree house. I soon found out otherwise. When I poked my head in through the doorway, I saw a web stretched from one wall to the next in the pattern of a wheel. The silk strands looked as strong as spokes. The spider in the hub had a seven-inch leg span. Bands of orange and black alternated along its spiny legs. I kept my mouth shut and eased back to the porch.

"What's wrong?" Conner grumbled, still in his tough-guy mode.

"You don't want to know." I looked for a way down other than through the main house. There wasn't one. The hatch in the floor was the only route to the ladder that spiraled down the trunk. I stepped back inside. The giant spider had a cone-shaped body. Legs like a skeleton's fingers. Deadly fangs. It fixed eight eyes on me and raised its front legs, as if to say, "One wrong move and you're mine."